Dangerous Waters
Strategies for Improving
Wellbeing at Work

STEPHEN WILLIAMS
Resource Systems, Harrogate, UK

And

LESLEY COOPER
IHC Strategy Ltd, London, UK

JOHN WILEY & SONS, LTD

Chichester · New York · Weinheim · Brisbane · Singapore · Toronto

Other Wiley Editorial Offices

John Wiley & Sons, Inc., 605 Third Avenue,
New York, NY 10158–0012, USA

WILEY-VCH Verlag GmbH, Pappelallee 3,
D-69469 Weinheim, Germany

Jacaranda Wiley Ltd, 33 Park Road, Milton,
Queensland 4064, Australia

John Wiley & Sons (Asia) Pte Ltd, 2 Clementi Loop #02–01,
Jin Xing Distripark, Singapore 129809

John Wiley & Sons (Canada) Ltd, 22 Worcester Road,
Rexdale, Ontario M9W 1L1, Canada

Library of Congress Cataloging-in-Publication Data
Williams, Steve, 1950–
    Dangerous waters : strategies for improving wellbeing at work /
Stephen Williams, Lesley Cooper.
        p.   cm. – (Wiley series in work, well-being, and stress)
    Includes bibliographical references and index.
    ISBN 0-471-98265-2
    1. Industrial hygiene.   2. Occupational diseases.   3. Health
promotion.   4. Work environment.   I. Cooper, Lesley.   II. Title.
III. Series.
    RC967.W54   1999   99–13346
    658.3'82–dc21   CIP

British Library Cataloguing in Publication Data

A catalogue record for this book is available from the British Library

ISBN 0-471-98265-2

Typeset in Palatino by BookEns Ltd, Royston, Herts.
Printed and bound in Great Britain by Biddles Ltd, Guildford and King's Lynn

This book is printed on acid-free paper responsibly manufactured from sustainable forestry, in which at
least two trees are planted for each one used for paper production.

Dangerous Waters

WILEY SERIES IN
WORK, WELL-BEING AND STRESS

Series Editor

Cary L. Cooper

Manchester School of Management
University of Manchester Institute of Science
and Technology, UK

Creating Healthy Work Organizations
Edited by Cary L. Cooper and Stephen Williams

Flexible Work Arrangements
*Benjamin H. Gottlieb, E. Kevin Kelloway and
Elizabeth J. Barham*

Contents

About the Authors

Stephen Williams
Dr Stephen Williams is the founder and Managing Director of Resource Systems, a human resource consultancy specialising in managing the consequences of organisational change, improving the quality of working life and helping organisations to increase the effectiveness of their recruitment and retention practices.

Stephen is an organisational psychologist with a background in HR management, working at director level in a variety of roles. His consultancy work includes advising major organisations in the UK and USA on the measurement and management of employee wellbeing and the development of appropriate interventions. He is also involved in the design and delivery of training programmes such as an innovative solution focused approach to team building and enhancing personal performance.

Stephen obtained his PhD for his work on the measurement of organisational stress and has developed a highly effective stress audit process. He is an Honorary Fellow of the Faculty of Occupational Medicine, the author of several books and numerous articles and a frequent speaker at conferences in the UK and overseas.

Stephen is married with one daughter and lives in Harrogate, North Yorkshire.

Lesley Cooper
Lesley Cooper is a specialist health management consultant, with particular expertise in the design and implementation of

workable strategies to reduce the cost of corporate ill health through a combination of primary prevention and targeted intervention.

Her models and approaches have grown from practical experience gained through close working with major UK employers to better understand and address the interrelationships between employee health, wellbeing and corporate performance. She has over fifteen years' experience in the corporate health care services sector, some of this time as Head of Health Management Consultancy for the health care company BUPA.

Lesley has particular expertise in the areas of occupational stress audit and management, health risk appraisal techniques and sickness absence management. She was one of the original developers of the integrated health management concept and has been heavily involved in recent years in promoting the benefits of the approach to the UK business community.

Lesley's business background includes training and development, corporate sales and sales management, strategic marketing, business development and management consultancy. She is the founder of IHC Strategy Ltd, a specialist consulting business based in central London.

Lesley is married with two daughters.

Introduction

Imagine your organisation is a sailing ship on a journey across the ocean. As you make your way towards your destination, you're aware of a variety of dangers that may affect your journey. Some of these dangers such as heavy seas, a lack of wind or poor navigation can slow you down or take you off course. These dangers are visible and, to some extent, predictable. You can forecast the weather and, by keeping a careful watch, you can see if the forecast is accurate or if conditions are changing. You can use a variety of instruments to measure your progress and get accurate information on your position, altering your course as necessary. You sail the ship by knowing where you want to go, taking frequent measurements to find out where you are, comparing these with previous measurements to monitor progress and making the appropriate changes to keep on course.

Now imagine that the sailing ship is equipped with all the latest technology, it has a global positioning system, computer-generated charts, radar systems and a link to clear and accurate weather forecasts. The crew have everything they need to respond to changes in conditions; they can change course, alter the sails, even run on engine power if necessary. However, the one thing that this ship doesn't have is a depth counter or any equipment that allows the crew to discover what lies below the surface of the ocean. They have a lot of information about the world above the surface but nothing about what's going on below. Most of the time this lack of information doesn't matter. The ship sails on through clear open waters and none of the crew sees, or is even aware of, the dangers that lie below the surface. They have no idea how close they've come to hitting a reef, the end of a sunken ship or being grounded in shallow water. All their attention is focused on the visible world. The captain and the crew know that there are risks below the surface of the sea — they've seen other ships sink and have come close to disaster on previous voyages. But, because they have no system for monitoring or recognising the dangers, they ignore them and carry on hoping that they will be lucky and stay afloat.

This is what it's like in organisations where employee wellbeing is ignored. The managers pursue their objectives and change things according to what they can see and what they can measure. The organisations' reporting systems are like the ship's radar and navigation systems; the managers use the systems to find out where they are and to identify what they need to change to get back on course. Most organisations have reasonably good systems for monitoring financial performance, quality issues, market forecasting and so on. Few of them have good systems for managing employee wellbeing. In the vast majority of organisations the 'people' systems are designed for the administration and processing of 'human resources' and have little to do with the management of people. The systems tell managers a lot about the jobs people have held, the training courses they've attended, and the performance rating they received. They tell them almost nothing of how people feel about the organisation or their work.

Think again about the sailing ship and imagine it's sailing toward a tropical island surrounded by a barrier reef. As the ship approaches the reef, the captain and crew can see the waves breaking on small outcrops of rock. They know that they have to get through the reef to reach their destination and they can see that this part of the voyage will be perhaps the most difficult. They know that the ship is at risk but they don't know the extent of the risk or how to avoid it. They change course to try to sail away from the obvious danger, the outcrops of rock, but if they are not careful they may end up putting themselves even more at risk as they sail onto the hidden reef.

In an organisation, staff turnover or sickness absence data is the manager's equivalent of seeing rocks sticking out of the water. They indicate hidden danger but only tell part of the story. Managers know there are problems when they find that their key people are leaving, that sickness absence seems to be getting worse, or that their accident rates are increasing, but few of them appreciate that these are only the most visible indicators of risk. In some organisations even these obvious warning signals are ignored completely and managers carry on as if there is nothing to cause them concern. It's as if the crew of the sailing ship is too busy checking the cargo or watching the weather to notice the danger ahead. So, in most organisations, the managers carry on managing. They focus on sales performance, improving quality, chasing cash flow, and developing new products until, as with the crew of the sailing ship, they discover they have made a fatal mistake. They are too busy concentrating on the things they can see and the things they can measure to notice they are in danger. They find out too late that it's not the things they've been managing that are the problem, it's the things they've been ignoring. It's the people issues that present the real danger, the loss of involvement, the lack of creativity, the 'couldn't care less' attitude to quality and service, the mistakes, the inefficiency, and the waste of opportunity. These are the things that the managers don't see; this is the hidden reef, the jagged rocks lying just below the waterline, this is the real danger. This is what sinks the ship.

This book is a guide through dangerous waters – it's written to help you understand and recognise the dangers that lie below the surface of your organisation. It's a guide to help you to identify and expose the hidden costs of employee wellbeing. Our intention is to raise awareness of these issues, to focus attention on the benefit of improving employee wellbeing and show how, if this area is neglected, it can, despite all the information systems, all the forecasting skills and all the business acumen, sink the organisation.

1
Why We Need a Strategy for Health and Wellbeing

We see the world as a series of impressions, fleeting glimpses of the reality that shapes our perceptions. We live through our beliefs, attitudes and assumptions and we make judgements on the basis of imperfect understanding. We sometimes think that we act rationally, that we make decisions based on facts and logic, but most of the time we just react to events without really understanding why. We bring our imperfect understanding of the world to work and, because work is supposed to be a rational activity, we pretend that we know what we're doing and try to justify our actions with evidence and reason. On the whole, we do the best we can with what we've got.

The nature of work in the late twentieth century is such that we don't really have time to think about what we've got. We have come to view management as a science; we collect information, we form hypotheses and we follow processes. We review our progress by measuring a variety of performance indicators and we change the way we do things or the things we do on the basis of our results. We read the management textbooks and we learn to become more focused, to concentrate on our core objectives, to increase our ability to add value. We miss the point.

We miss the point that the workplace is made up of people and most people don't go to work thinking about how they can maximise shareholder value or achieve corporate objectives.

They go to work thinking about themselves, their families, their friends, their hobbies, their interests, world events, or even the TV programmes they watched last night. They think about the impact work has on their lives and they think about their jobs, their colleagues, their managers, their tasks, and their futures. We miss the point that when people come to work, the whole person comes to work, not just the part that does the job. When we manage people we manage the whole person. When we employ someone we employ a person, a fellow human being. We don't hire a worker, we bring a person into our workplace. We bring them in to do a job, to perform a task and, presumably, to add value to our activities. We may or may not believe that 'people are our most important asset' but if we didn't need people we wouldn't employ them.

This book is about the nature of work and the relationship between the employer and the employee. It is based on the premise that people matter. That they add value to the business and that the better the people, the better the business. In writing this book we have drawn on our experience of working with people in a wide variety of organisations: public and private, big and small, successful and not so successful. We have had the opportunity, over many years, to observe and measure the difference that people make to their employers and the impact that organisations have on people. We believe that people do make a difference and organisational success goes hand in hand with individual success. If you take care of your people they will take care of you. Our experience shows that most organisations miss many of the key people issues. They 'surface manage' the people side of the business and fail to maximise the contribution that their people can make.

In this book we want to show that it is possible to get below the surface of the people issues, understand what really matters and, by improving wellbeing at work, simultaneously improve organisational performance and personal fulfilment.

Organisations have highly sophisticated systems for managing their activities. They use these systems to integrate the data they collect on every aspect of business. Computer software provides 'dashboard' measures to analyse cash flow in real time, measure production output in minute detail, track each shipment mile by mile, monitor the rate of return on investment and so on. There is almost no aspect of business that isn't measured, monitored, integrated with other data, and modelled. The measurements are used to predict future demand, change product lines and prices, decide what will sell, identify cost savings, and make endless other sophisticated changes to the business. Billions of dollars are invested in the latest generation of management tools such as Enterprise Resource Planning software to give managers ever more detailed information about the business. There is a general acceptance that in order to manage something it must first be measured. The argument for increasing investment in management systems is that the more detailed the measurement, the more data that can be collected and integrated, the better the understanding of the business and the greater the improvement in efficiency.

Contrast this with the investment in information about the staff. Organisations know almost nothing about their employees apart from the basic details necessary for personnel or payroll administration. The lack of attention to understanding the people issues is demonstrated by a scan through human resource or personnel management journals. There are systems for personnel administration, sickness absence, recruitment tracking, training needs analysis, time recording, and performance monitoring. All of these systems are concerned with personnel administration or process management. These systems tell the organisation when an employee joined, what he is paid, when he was last promoted, when he last had a day off, how many hours he worked last week. They don't show if people are happy, enjoy their jobs, feel they're making a useful contribution, or feel fulfilled. Some organisations have information collected once a year from an anonymous employee opinion survey, but in most organisations there is almost no current information on how individuals feel about their work or their business. Personnel systems miss the point – people don't need to be administered, they need to be involved. We're constantly told that people matter, but it appears that they don't matter enough to be treated as individuals.

The book is structured to show why organisations cannot ignore the world outside the workplace, why changes in society place a burden of responsibility on employers that they cannot ignore. It shows the weakness in a superficial analysis of

Figure 1.1   *People are our most important asset (Copyright 1993 United Feature Syndicate, Inc. Reproduced with permission)*

employee wellbeing and how getting below the surface can reveal the true benefits of a healthy workforce. The book then outlines the case for a strategic approach to managing health, shows how measurement tools aid understanding, and describes a series of interventions to improve individual and organisational wellbeing.

The journey to workplace health starts with a leap of faith. It requires a belief that people are more important than carbon paper (Figure 1.1). That people work more effectively, more creatively and more productively when they are stimulated, respected and fulfilled and that, in the words of Robert Rosen, 'healthy people make healthy companies'.

HEALTH AND WELLBEING

Good health is assumed to be the absence of illness or injury. Provided that you are not in pain, don't have a disease, and are not showing symptoms of illness, then you are healthy. While we know that this cannot be right, as many diseases are 'silent' during their early stages, and others, such as psychological illness, may be hidden for years, in reality this is the approach taken by most employers concerning their employees' health. In most organisations the management of health is the management of illness. If people are not physically ill, then they must be well. If they are present for work, then they are not sick. Managing health at this level is simple and straightforward. Make sure the employee has a 'genuine' illness and is not a malingerer, then leave it to the health services to make them better as quickly as possible. It's as simple as that. There is no need to make health management a high priority for the organisation or develop a health strategy. This attitude can be summarised as: 'We can't stop people getting ill and, as long as they don't have too much time off work, there isn't a problem.' The first step in developing a strategic approach for the management of health is to broaden this narrow view, move away from the focus on illness, and help managers to understand that they have a significant influence on wellbeing at work.

Dimensions of Health

The absence of physical illness is too limiting a definition for our understanding of wellbeing. Physical health is one of the components of wellbeing but the absence of physical illness does not, of itself, make a healthy individual. Other aspects of health need to be taken into consideration. In addition to physical health, the most frequently cited are social health and psychological health. This combination of physical, psychological and social health forms the basis of the World Health Organisation (WHO) definition of health. Looking at health in the workplace, the WHO and the International Labour Office (ILO) define the purpose of occupational health as follows:

> The promotion and maintenance of the highest degree of physical, mental and social wellbeing of workers in all occupations by prevention of departures from health and controlling risk.

An individual can be described as being physically healthy when they're free of disease and injury; they are psychologically healthy when they have self-esteem, are resilient, and are not anxious or depressed. Socially healthy people enjoy good relationships, have a variety of interests and coexist comfortably with other people. Any discussion of employee wellbeing needs to take these aspects of health, and their potential interrelationships, into account.

Economic Health

Defining wellbeing as the presence of good physical, psychological and social health broadens our understanding of the issues but still doesn't go far enough. We believe that a fourth dimension — economic health — should also be included. Population statistics show a clear relationship between economic prosperity and individual health. People in richer countries tend to live longer and have healthier lives than people in poor countries. Economic health does not mean economic wealth but it does mean having enough to maintain the necessities of life. In an organisational context, economic health is an important consideration. It's difficult to see how employees can be regarded as healthy or enjoy wellbeing if they're living in poverty or are being exploited by working long hours in unpleasant conditions for a meagre wage. A sweatshop is not a healthy work environment.

Economically Healthy Organisations

There is a strong link between the financial success of the organisation and the wellbeing of the employee. It could be argued that the economic prosperity of an organisation might also be a predictor of employee health. It presupposes that, in order to promote wellbeing at work, the organisation has to prosper. Our experience shows that economically healthy organisations are the ones most able to provide a working environment that promotes the physical, psychological and social health of their employees. We also believe that this investment in wellbeing is repaid, as healthy employees will produce greater economic prosperity for their employer.

Finally our definition needs to include environmental health. Although this may be seen as a component of the other health dimensions, we believe that it is such an important factor that it should be treated as a separate issue. Environmental health means control of hazardous substances, noise levels, a comfortable temperature and adequate space, light and ventilation.

These five factors, i.e. physical, psychological and social health, plus economic health and environmental health, interact to provide the building blocks of employee wellbeing; they emphasise the positive aspects of wellbeing rather than the avoidance of illness and show that the various components of wellbeing are interrelated. Organisations have a responsibility to promote and maintain positive health. In order to do so they need to understand what wellness looks like and what happens when the workforce is not well.

Work on Health and Health on Work

Concern for employee health at work has traditionally focused on two major areas: the effect of the work itself on the health of the employee and the employee's fitness for work. The effect of work on health is concerned with the risk to the individual of suffering ill health due to workplace hazards or dangers. Historically this has focused on physical health risks such as exposures to chemicals, dust, noise, toxic environments and so on. More recently, employees' mental wellbeing has become a cause for concern, with occupational stress now being seen as a major occupational health hazard. Fitness for work is about employees' ability to do the job without damage to themselves or others.

But, as above, the issue is broader than this. Employees are subject to a myriad of pressures and influences that have the potential to impact on their ability to function while at work. Many of these are not 'traditional' occupational health issues, and many more of them originate outside of the workplace and are therefore not, on the face of it, the employer's responsibility. But either by themselves or in combination they have the potential to become real health issues that undermine the employees' ability to do their jobs to the level employers would want. Health at work should therefore refer to the dynamic interaction between work and work-related process and, at the very least, physical, psychological and social health.

On the left-hand side of Figure 1.2 are the 'traditional' concerns of occupational health: physical health risks, associated with exposure to toxins, poor ergonomics and so on, social health risks typified by workplace bullying and harassment and finally psychological risks such as occupational stress and post-traumatic stress syndrome. All these are issues that most occupational health practitioners will be closely focused on and are clearly to do with work affecting health.

On the right-hand side of the model are the some of the less obvious ways that health can affect work. Physical health issues

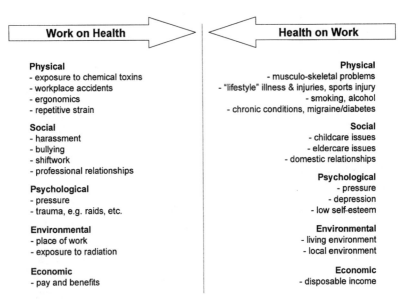

Figure 1.2   *Work on health–health on work*

such as lower back pain, migraine and diabetes are not of necessity 'created' by the work, but they will affect the employee's ability to attend for work or function well while there. Similarly, under the social category, problems with children or elderly relatives are not 'of the employer's making' but will affect the employee's ability to come to work or be productive. Finally, under psychological health, are the not inconsiderable threats to attendance and effectiveness from poor pressure management and low morale.

The point is that many of these issues are not immediately apparent to the employer, and, until fairly recently at least, there has been little legislation in place to encourage employers to understand more about them. But whether immediately apparent or not, *they are* occupational health issues because they affect the employee's ability either to get to work or to function well while there.

The Positive Impact of Work on Health

When considering the work–health relationship, it's important to remember that the two are not incompatible or mutually exclusive. As studies of the effects of unemployment show, work can have a positive influence on health. One of the biggest dangers in the assumption that work and health are incompatible is a managerial attitude that says there is a conflict between productive working practices and safe or healthy working practices. It's still quite easy to find managers, some in very senior positions, who believe that health and safety gets in the way of profits and any concern for employee wellbeing will inevitably reduce productivity. There is a clear expectation that occupational health professionals or people that are involved in employee wellbeing will always want to make things easier for the employee at the expense of the employer. They will advocate fewer working hours, more breaks, less demanding work. The personnel professional, the occupational physician or the caring manager will seek to protect the health and safety of the employees and is right to insist that safe working practices are followed and health and safety issues are not subservient to profits. However, in the vast majority of circumstances, protecting employee health will not adversely affect the productivity of the workforce.

Visible and Hidden Health Issues

The conventional view of employee wellbeing is the view of the partially sighted. Managers see only the most obvious manifestation of employee wellbeing but not the complete picture. What's visible above the surface may indicate that there are problems below but, without better information, it's very hard to take corrective action. This concept of visible and hidden health issues is important. The barrier reef analogy illustrates that not all of the health issues that concern an employer are easy to see. Figure 1.3 shows some of the issues involved and how some of these are visible to the organisation and others are hidden from view.

Above the water-line are staff turnover and sickness absence, the most obvious signs of poor health and wellbeing. These are clearly visible to the employer; staff turnover because there is a requirement to exit interview or replace a valuable employee and sickness absence because the employee is not present, work requires redistribution or temporary cover is required. The costs

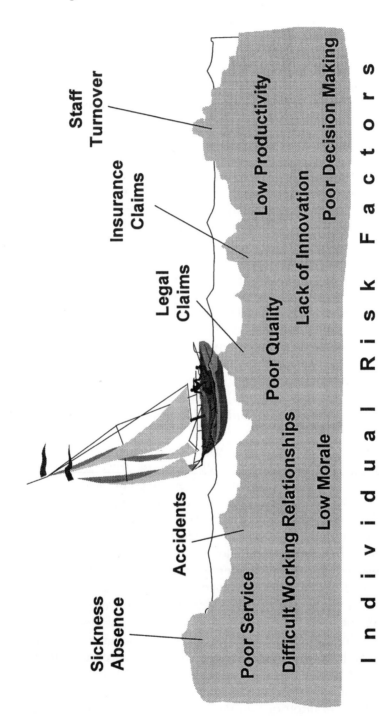

Staff Turnover

Insurance Claims

Legal Claims

Accidents

Sickness Absence

Low Productivity

Poor Decision Making

Lack of Innovation

Poor Quality

Difficult Working Relationships

Low Morale

Poor Service

I n d i v i d u a l   R i s k   F a c t o r s

Figure 1.3   *Visible and hidden costs of poor employee wellbeing*

associated with these issues, though often hard to calculate, are also clear to see. Temporaries cost money. So do advertisements or agency fees for new staff. The other issues that appear above the water-line include accidents, legal claims, and insurance claims such as employer liability and private health insurance. These issues may not always be seen as manifestations of ill health and poor wellbeing and usually only come to the surface as isolated 'one off' incidents. They are examples of problems that lie hidden below the water-line until they grow to a point where they can be seen.

Beneath the surface of the water there are many more problems that are linked to poor wellbeing. Most of these are invisible to the employer and many of them are also hidden from the employee. Some of these issues lie just below the surface, sometimes visible, sometimes hidden. They are like outcrops of rock that are only revealed at low tide. The rest of the time they are hidden from view. For example, poor customer service may not be a problem until competition in the market means that customers demand more attention and take their business elsewhere if they don't get it. The depths also contain other, perhaps unexpected, dangers. There will be accidents, bullying, harassment and other events that take place but go unrecorded. So the manager remains unaware of them and may even be causing them. There will also be existing health issues of which the employer is unaware. The employee may have a condition that would justify an absence day, which would make the issue more visible, but they choose to 'soldier on' and so the condition of the employee remains undetected for the time being. In certain circumstances the employee may not even be aware that she or he is either socially, psychologically or physically ill and so neither party can see the danger.

Moving further underwater we reach the base of the reef. This represents the individual risk factors, the health and lifestyle risks to which all employees are exposed. In the same way that coral grows from millions of tiny organisms, so the visible and hidden costs of health are made up from a myriad of individual health risks. Being aware of the existence of these risks is important for our understanding of how employee health can and should be managed. Most diseases develop slowly in the presence of observable risk factors, some of which are genetic, some environmental and some behavioural. Some of the factors can therefore be influenced and some cannot. The way each individual reacts to the work environment and their unique cocktail of health factors determines the way in which health and wellbeing issues manifest themselves. Understanding the interaction between the individual and the workplace requires knowledge of both the individual health factors and of the organisational factors that either develop or destroy workplace wellbeing.

We shall return to this later, but for now the point is that a great many of the factors that determine the future health of employees are hidden from view, 'below the waves'. At least that is where they start. Initially hidden, the issues slowly move towards the surface where they then become much easier to see. Unfortunately for both the employee and employer, by the time they reach the surface and become visible it is too late. The employee has resigned, the legal claim has been made or the insurance premiums have doubled. This slow migration of employee health issues from 'risk' to 'reality' is often overlooked, and time, money and effort are expended dealing with the effects, not the causes. Because many of the issues are not immediately apparent, most of the attention often goes on to managing what has already happened. Rather than looking for ways to reduce the number of episodes of ill health among the workforce, attention is usually focused on trying to limit both the direct and indirect impact of the illness on the company. Following our analogy, the issues are managed at the surface when they become visible, not below the water-line where they start. All the emphasis is placed on loss reduction and damage limitation rather than proactive health management for positive gain.

This shift in emphasis from *reactive* to *proactive* healthcare management is fundamental to our understanding of how to improve wellbeing at work. We explore this theme in more detail in Chapter 7, but the following example illustrates how the model works in relation to occupational stress.

Stress is the negative outcome of an imbalance between the perceived pressure or demands on an individual and their ability to cope. Most of the early symptoms of this imbalance are hidden, so even the employee may not be aware that they are suffering from stress in the early stages. But as the pressure builds, the issue comes closer to the surface, until it bursts up from under the water to become visible as an error of judgement, a sharp exchange of words with a superior or repeated episodes of absence. All employee health and wellbeing issues are continuous, but their true cost and manageability depends on the point at which they are made manifest. The problem is further compounded by the fact that often the issue does not become noticeable until it is already too late to manage and even then what is seen is only a fraction of what has already gone wrong. Scanning the horizon for signs of ill health is not enough. You need to look below the surface if you are to really understand the health and wellbeing of your employees.

SICKNESS ABSENCE

How Big an Issue is It?

In many organisations sickness absence is regarded as the quantifiable measure of corporate health. Indeed, all too often, sickness absence is the only health measure. As *the* most visible manifestation of employee ill health, the issue has risen in prominence in recent years. This is partly due to it being easier to observe and monitor than other ill health indicators and, in the UK, the government's decision to remove the employer's right to reclaim statutory sick pay has been another catalyst for closer scrutiny of absence.

Absence is a large and growing issue. In 'Missing Out' – the 1998 absence and labour turnover survey from the Confederation of British Industry (CBI) – the direct cost to UK businesses is reported to be in the region of £11 billion per annum. The CBI reports that in 1997 there were 8.4 working days lost on average per employee, which is equivalent to an absence rate of 3.7%, up from 3.4% in a comparable study in 1994 and unchanged from 1996. The estimated number of days lost to sickness absence in 1997 were 197 million, an increase of 10 million over the previous survey. The average absence level for non-manual workers was 6.8 days (down from 8 days in the previous year's survey) and 10.8 days for manual workers, slightly up from a figure of 9.7 in 1996. These statistics reveal a large and significant cost to employers and to the UK economy, but they are a massive understatement of the true cost of ill health.

Attitudes to Sickness Absence

Until fairly recently there was a great deal of inertia about managing absence, as well as a degree of ignorance about the attendant costs. Many companies were found to have little awareness of what the overall direct costs might be and even less interest in actively managing the issue.

Our work with companies has involved an analysis of attitudes and approaches towards corporate health care, including the management of sickness absence. In particular, our research seeks to establish the structure of employee health care benefits and services within organisations and better understand why they make these investments.

The results are often surprising. Generally speaking, until recently, awareness of sickness absence levels has been low and few organisations have robust systems for measurement. Absence has almost invariably been seen as the local responsibility of line management and there is often deep scepticism that levels of sickness can be influenced in any major way. Monitoring of absence has often been regarded as essentially an administrative process, which has little use other than at local management level and is certainly seen as detached from the commercial considerations of the business.

However, interest in the subject has grown dramatically in recent years. Most human resources (HR) departments we speak to now have recently been tasked with investigating absence trends more fully. Most interestingly, the impetus for this seems to be coming from finance departments, but there is still little awareness among those involved regarding what commercial use this information might be put to once collected.

Perhaps the most startling observation from our discussions with UK employers is the scepticism that exists in nearly all companies that even armed with 'the facts' it will be possible to reduce levels of sickness absence. Paradoxically though, most of the companies we have spoken to are investing considerable sums in health services that will have an effect on employee absence levels. Typically these take the form of health insurance or health screening, but these benefits are provided more from 'tradition' than any attempt to influence health outcomes. There are rarely any links being made between the cost of employee ill health and the purchase of these health investments. If a business justification for their purchase has been thought out, this does not appear to be based on benefits conferred from reduced employee absence.

Despite this, as mentioned above, there has been a relative explosion in the amount of market activity and interest in the area. Invitations to participate in conferences on sickness absence seem to fall from HR and other business journals faster than you can get yourself registered. Most HR and occupational health (OH) personnel know the published CBI absence figures and many of the companies involved in the initial survey are now heavily involved in getting closer to the real extent of their absence problem. This is good news. But most interestingly, the majority of employers *still* fail to make the connection between the cost of absence and the current cost and positioning of health investments. Employers are investing significant amounts of money on health benefits, but they are not apparently doing this with the conscious aim of reducing absence by improving employee health. These are regarded as two non-related activities.

Sickness absence is a huge and costly issue, but if many of the platform speakers at the conferences are anything to go by, the current answers lie more in tightening up the rules and looking for the truants, than in better understanding the reasons for it. They advocate managing absence by policing sickness, not by improving wellness.

OTHER ILL HEALTH COSTS

The direct cost of employee ill health is observable, above the surface, at many other points. What follows is by no means an exhaustive list.

Ill health retirements (IHRs), whether they are few or many, are a significant cost to the company. One UK clearing bank decided to embark on a more formalised approach to employee health management on the basis of their cost experience in this area alone. The pension costs are considerable in their own right, and the more senior the employee the more noticeable the cost. But these are not the only expenses. The employee's reduced efficiency, as their illness developed and necessitated increasingly frequent absences from work, will have made a mark on the company. Their ultimate severance from the organisation and all business activities they were contributing to will also have made an impact. Add to this the cost of recruiting and retraining a replacement, as well as the value of the lost intellectual property, and the balance sheet looks bleak indeed. A review of IHRs will often show that early identification and closer management of the underlying medical condition could have mitigated its effect and so prevented the premature retirement and all attendant human and commercial costs.

Employer liability insurance is another area for scrutiny. Liability premiums have been rising for a number of years and some of the major UK insurers are looking towards discounting the premiums for companies who can demonstrate a formal commitment to maintaining employee health. Conversely, organisations who take a less proactive stance on employee health are experiencing higher premium increases. If the less visible employee health risks are not properly understood, there is increased opportunity for the employer to unwittingly place the employee at risk. Ignorance is increasingly seen by the courts as no excuse, and the dimensions of just one or two claims against the employer (not withstanding the potential impact of damaged public relations) can very easily run into tens if not hundreds of thousands of pounds.

Employee litigation is also on the increase. Not so long ago an employee who developed work-related upper limb disorder might stop doing the work, because it hurt too much to continue and think no more of it. Now employees are much more health aware and the chances of employers being involved in an expensive lawsuit are considerably greater. The injury does not have to be physical either. Bullying, harassment, stress and other aspects of psychological ill health are becoming increasingly common. As above, the direct costs can be quite substantial without taking into account the damage done to the employer's reputation.

In counting the cost of employee ill health let us not forget the increased *potential* for accidents. Certainly when an employee is unwell there is a greater chance of an accident occurring at work, with its attendant human and financial costs. Slips, trips, falls, breaks, strains and all other obvious injuries are easy to account for and are health costs. Less immediately apparent, but just as damaging, are episodes of 'intellectual accident' where the employee was feeling so under par that they made an error of judgement that cost the company far in excess of the cost of their sick pay while they recovered at home.

Another insurance-related health cost concerns private medical insurance. Few involved in the annual negotiation of private medical insurance plans will have failed to notice the apparently inexorable rise in premium levels. The factors driving medical insurance costs are complex in their own right, but in the vast majority of cases the larger corporate plans are priced with reference to previous years' claims experience. Many employee health issues, be they driven by the effect of 'work on health' or more to do with 'health on work', find their way into these claim figures.

It sounds obvious that these health insurance claims should be counted as employee health costs but surprisingly often they are not. Decisions are sometimes taken to 'move' an insurance contract to a new provider, frequently on the basis of cost saving, with little attention paid to the underlying health issues that are driving the claims. Re-negotiations of the contract focus on the issues of price and service delivery, which are important, but employee health rarely figures for long in any discussion. When you consider that health insurance premiums are often among the largest value employee benefits provided, this disassociation with health seems strange.

Staff Turnover

Staff turnover is perhaps the most visible of these other health costs. It is an obvious cost to the organisation, but may not always be associated with health or wellbeing. In our analogy, staff turnover is a piece of the reef projecting out of the water that is part of a much larger outcrop just below the surface (see Figure 1.3). Most people who choose to leave their employer do so because they are dissatisfied with some aspect of the organisation, their colleagues, their pay or their work. Very few really leave because they have been 'made an offer they can't refuse'. The decision to seek alternative employment or follow up a call from a head-hunter starts with a sense of frustration or a lack of fulfilment, a sense that there may be something better out there. It usually takes several months or even years before an employee actually gets round to resigning. For all that time the organisation has a problem, perhaps a minor one of the employee being a bit distracted or not quite so committed, perhaps a major one of switching off altogether. The difficulty for the organisation is that until notice to quit is given, there is no visible sign of a problem. In most cases, when it becomes visible it is too late.

The cost of staff turnover, like sickness absence, is compounded further by the employee being absent from work either temporarily if they are 'off sick' or permanently if they have resigned or taken early retirement. Their absence will often necessitate the additional cost of temporary cover, which in a large organisation can run into hundreds of thousands of pounds in a year. This is good business for recruitment and temporary staff companies, but represents a significant area of avoidable cost. For some organisations the cost and volume of temporary cover has risen so dramatically that sign-off at director level is now required before temporary replacements can be contracted in.

THE HIDDEN HEALTH ISSUES

The previous section highlighted some of the more obvious costs of health and these will be examined in more detail in later chapters. But what of the hidden costs, the issues that lie below the surface which, for most organisations, are rarely associated with health? These issues often manifest themselves as morale or performance issues; they are signs of organisational malaise and indicators of poor employee wellbeing.

Industrial disputes such as strikes are an obvious example of when the hidden issues of poor wellbeing become visible. Tension and confrontation in the workplace damages employees as well as the employer. Strikes or lockouts have a direct link to economic wellbeing and, by emphasising an 'us and them' approach, also damage social health. Industrial disputes are both a source of pressure for those involved and a manifestation of stress. The ensuing psychological and physical health damage is all too real for many people. The problem with linking disputes to health and wellbeing is one of cause and effect. In our experience, industrial disputes occur when wellbeing is ignored. Issues that should be addressed in a co-operative manner become confrontational and trust disappears. In many cases, greater awareness and better communication on both sides could have avoided the dispute.

Fairness at work is another aspect of employee wellbeing that is not usually associated with health. These issues concern problems with individuals at work. They include discrimination, harassment, bullying and favouritism. As with our previous examples, most of the time these are hidden from view, often well down in the murky depths where individual managers, supervisors or co-workers damage or destroy the lives of those around them. The health links are clear, from economic disadvantage or social isolation to psychological or physical distress. By the time these issues come to the surface there can be considerable damage to the individual and enormous cost to the organisation.

SUMMARY

All these employee health issues are real and they all affect the ability of the employee to perform effectively at work. They have an impact on performance, productivity and profit. Many of them are hidden from the employer's view, but that does not make them any less dangerous if they are ignored. The issues need to be made visible and managed before they get out of control. Improving employee wellbeing is not a simple or easy process – it takes time, effort, resources and, perhaps most importantly, a willingness to act. Action stems from understanding and the following chapters show why wellbeing is such a key issue and offer strategies for effective intervention.

2
Wellbeing in the Changing World

We live in a changing world. Change pervades every aspect of our lives. Changes in society, economics, technology and the environment combine to produce dramatic changes in the world of work, with profound implications for both the employee and the employer. In the words of Charles Handy, 'Change is not what it used to be'. Change is discontinuous. To survive and prosper in a dramatically changing world organisations need to understand change and have the flexibility to adapt quickly, effectively and appropriately. These changes affect how people work, where they work, when they work, what they do at work, and who does the work. Managing employee wellbeing involves understanding these issues and recognising that they are all interdependent. Change affects people and the ability of each individual to manage change in their lives affects organisational success. You cannot manage organisational change without understanding personal change.

SOCIAL AND DEMOGRAPHIC CHANGES

Change in Family Life

There is a hidden assumption in many organisations that our employees go home each evening to the 'cereal packet norm' of Mum, Dad and two children, but this is increasingly not the case.

The proportion of 'traditional' households in the UK, comprising two parents with dependent children has fallen over the last 35 years from 38% in 1961 to 25% in 1996–97. Lone parents now head around one-fifth of all families with dependent children in the UK, nearly three times the proportion in 1971. Much of this has to do with our increasing divorce rate, with the UK having the second highest divorce rate in the EU at 2.9 per thousand population. In the USA, 52% of first marriages end in divorce. There has been growth since 1986 in one-parent families, partly due to an increase in the number of single women choosing to be lone mothers.

Of the 80% or so of families that are still the traditional shape, the dynamics of those families are changing at a rapid pace. Whether for reasons of financial necessity or not, increasing numbers of women are entering the workplace, delaying having children in order to stay there longer and, when they do have children, having fewer of them. To put this into some sort of context, women born in 1936 had an average of 1.9 children by the time they were 30, compared with 1.3 children to women born in 1966.

Dual Career Couples

Just over three-fifths of married couples of working age with dependent children are 'dual income' families. This represents a growth from just over half in the early 1980s. In contrast, the proportion of families where only the man is working fell from around 40% in the early 1980s to about 25% in 1996–97.

Economic activity rates measure the percentage of the population which is in the labour force, either working or seeking and available for work. Economic activity rates for women have been increasing since the early 1970s, with the rate for men falling slightly. Of men aged 16–64, 84% were economically active in 1997, compared with 91% in 1971. But for women aged 16–59, 71% were economically active in 1997, compared with 56% in 1971.

This trend looks set to continue as our ageing population draws more and more women into the workplace. As greater financial independence becomes the achievable norm for women, fewer and fewer will believe it 'inappropriate' to return to work after the birth of their children, to the extent that staying at home will appear the unusual form of behaviour.

Work and Motherhood

The concept of 'working mother' has become commonplace but, behind the considerable practical difficulties that may be involved in pursuing both professional and maternal roles, there are other issues. Although many female employees look forward to the day when they can return to work, the actual transition back into the workplace can be quite traumatic. In addition to the inevitable 'pull' of leaving the child with a carer, they frequently find that there is a need to adjust their expectations of what can realistically be achieved in the workplace in the first few months.

For those who habitually worked late before their children were born, there are new and stressful situations to be dealt with. Leaving a meeting in full flow at 5 o'clock sharp in order to battle through traffic and reach the nursery or child-minder on time can create a sense of powerlessness and lack of control over events. They may feel that their colleagues no longer view them as 'full time' or serious about their job, while they in themselves have never been more determined to make a contribution.

In reality, these changed external circumstances can actually facilitate a 'smarter' contribution, purely because the working day has become more time limited. To 'get it all done', time management skills are often noticed to improve and productivity during those finite working hours can increase. Yet few organisations actively rehabilitate working parents back into the world of work, and not doing so can have profound implications for the wellbeing of the employees involved in making the transition. Without open acknowledgement by employers that some employees' circumstances may have altered, demoralisation and demotivation can quickly set in and the working parent slowly convinces themselves that you can't, in fact, 'have it all'.

For the previously very driven and competitive employees, the view becomes if you can't play and win there's no point in playing. The very employees organisations most want to keep, because of their drive and enthusiasm, could easily leave because they do not feel they can contribute on the same terms as before and that therefore they do not have a role.

Gender Wars

It is not just the employer who is affected by the growth in dual career families. The increasing number of women who return to work after the birth of their children, or who choose not to have children at all but pursue a career instead, has implications for their partners too. Whether we realise it or not, the old gender roles of husband at work and wife at home have underpinned the world of work for some time. The ritual of returning from work to a family setting, where food and drink have already been prepared and the day can be 'laid to rest', has provided an antidote to the stresses and strains of predominantly male working lives. The situation now is rather different. Returning home from the office or factory, many men are likely to find an empty house and a hastily scribbled note directing them to the local take-away. A considerable number of them will also not come upon this note until after they have collected children from their carers and wrestled them through tea, bath, bedtime story and finally bed.

One of the many social implications of women entering the workplace is that the domestic support mechanism, that enabled many male employees to cope with their own increased pressure, has disappeared, in some cases almost overnight.

As has been said many times before, the drive for women to 'break through the glass ceiling' while also looking after dependent children and relatives is often achieved at great personal cost to themselves and their family. Not surprisingly, the intense pressure as both parties try to align all their often conflicting needs and wants alongside the practical matters of caring for dependants, places an intolerable strain on their relationship with their partners. There is ample evidence for this coming through from data gathered by employee counselling services. Where employers are providing such a service, relationship counselling is often the most frequently requested part of the programme.

Lack of Community Support and Problems of Social Isolation

It is not just changes to the structure of the employee's immediate family that are significant in this context. The increase in mobility means that people will move house several times in their lifetime. This means that along with the increasing number of either single parent families, or families with both partners working, we also have an increasing sense of isolation from remaining members of the extended family and other people in the community.

Not so long ago, the majority of people would grow up, leave home, set up house and bring up their children within a few streets or, at the most, a few miles of their parents, grandparents, brothers, sisters and cousins. They would live in a community with those they had known since childhood, with a wide range of people they could turn to for support or help. This help ranges from sharing the care of children, caring for the elderly, getting the shopping for someone who is ill, taking the children to school and so on. The community gave people a sense of belonging, a sense of place and, perhaps more importantly, an extended network of people who could help out in all sorts of ways whenever that help was needed.

The situation is very different for many people in today's workplace. The average employee, and certainly the average manager, technician or professionally qualified employee, is likely to be living in a different city or different part of the country from their family. They may have a wide circle of friends, but those friends may also have spread all over the country or overseas and they are unlikely to have been in their current location for long enough to have become part of a mutually supportive network. If, as is increasingly the case, both partners are working, they're probably working long hours, and by the time they've managed the house, spent time with each other and the children, there just aren't enough hours to get to know people in their community. They live their lives on the brink of disaster. As long as everything goes smoothly they can survive, but all it takes is one small problem, an unforeseen incident, and the lack of support leaves them unable to cope.

Employers put Policies before People

Some employers have such little understanding of the pressures that social isolation places on their staff and their families that they impose policies which make things worse. A large multinational food company demonstrated this point when they decided to relocate one of their senior export sales managers. The sales manager had been with the company for almost ten years and was one of their most successful export managers. He worked hard, produced good results and was willing to travel wherever and whenever he was needed. He would usually be away from home for three weeks out of four and he, his wife and family had adjusted to the nature of his work and, although they would have preferred slightly less time away, were quite happy.

The problems arose when the company went through a reorganisation and the export sales group reported to a different divisional head in another location. The company insisted that the sales manager had to relocate to the new head office, despite the fact that he spent most of his time working overseas. They failed to realise that what enabled the sales manager to do his job was that his wife and family were very settled in their present home. They had family and good friends within a few miles, the children enjoyed their school and moving would have meant leaving behind all of the support systems that enabled them to cope with the sales manager's frequent absences. The sales manager tried repeatedly to explain his situation to the company and offered a number of alternatives that would enable him to carry out his export sales role, attend whatever meetings he needed to at head office and not relocate his family. The company was adamant that everyone should adhere to the relocation policy and would not accept a compromise. After several months of arguing the point and an enormous amount of distress to the sales manager, his wife and his family, the sales manager resigned without another job to go to. He lost a job he enjoyed with a company he liked. The company lost a valuable member of staff with ten years of knowledge, contacts and success. They both lost because the company put policies before people.

Elder Care Issues

Another striking feature of the changes in population demographics is the so-called 'greying' of the population. People are
living longer, birth rates are falling and the average age of the
population in the developed countries is on the increase.
Employees at the most productive stage in their lives in terms
of workplace productivity are increasingly having to balance
elder care responsibilities with their child care role.

Of course this is not news − these trends have been evident
for some time. But what is significant is that this increase in the
number of dual income families, combined with the growing
complexity of their caring responsibilities and in some cases
correspondingly shrinking social support, has far reaching
implications for the employer. Increased job mobility means
that many professional workers will have moved away from their
parents and can no longer just 'pop round the corner' to see if
everything is as it should be. Elder care issues will inevitably
affect a significant proportion of the workforce and employees of
both sexes will need to demand some measure of empathy from
their employer as they juggle these frequently conflicting
demands on their time, energy and commitment.

The problem with lack of support is illustrated by the story of
a professional couple in their late 30s, Jeff and Alice. They have
two teenage children and live in a pleasant part of North London.
They both work in demanding jobs and have organised their
lives so that they both spend about 50 hours a week at the office,
bring work home most nights and spend most of Sunday evening
reading through papers and preparing for the week ahead. They
no longer have a lot of time for socialising and find it difficult to
attend as many of the children's events as they would like.
Although Jeff and Alice spend most of their time feeling worn
out, they don't think about it too much and just about manage to
keep everything going.

Matters came to a head when Alice's elderly mother was taken
ill. Her mother lived alone on the south coast and had been in
reasonably good health. However, she collapsed one day and
was taken to hospital. The hospital phoned Alice and she and Jeff
dropped everything and spent two and a half hours driving
down to see Alice's mother. When they got to the hospital they

found that she seemed to be all right and, after spending a little time with her, drove home again. The first time this happened it caused a few problems but they got by. Unfortunately, Alice's mother continued to have problems. She collapsed again a few days later and once more Jeff and Alice rushed down to be with her. Once again she got better and they returned. Over the next few months the situation deteriorated and Jeff and Alice found it impossible to manage the children, their jobs and Alice's mother's ill health. Their work suffered, their health suffered, the children suffered, and their relationship broke down under the strain.

Jeff and Alice's story isn't unusual. In their case it was primarily a problem of looking after an elderly relative. For other people, their children have difficulties at school or there are problems with child-minders, or there is illness in the family. In all of these cases, the combination of busy lives and the absence of reliable support means that resources are stretched too thin and something has to give. It may be the relationship, the job or the person's health; often it is all three.

WHY THESE SOCIAL ISSUES MATTER

Employers that fail to recognise the pressures that change in society places on individuals cannot therefore be providing the support that's so often lacking in the community. By failing to anticipate the needs of their staff they are effectively assuming that social responsibilities, whether for the elderly or the young, are the individual's problem and that they should take care of it themselves, not bring it to the workplace.

The additional pressure that these dual, or sometimes triple, roles place on employees as they seek to perform adequately on several fronts simultaneously should not be underestimated. When we consider that 'adequate performance' on any front is unlikely to be considered enough, then it is easy to see how the pressures can build until they become overwhelming.

Despite these trends being self-evident, remarkably few organisations make specific provision in their health care planning to aid their employees in balancing these conflicting demands. This seems to be for two reasons. First, as topics they do not often find their way into health planning discussions because they are not seen as health issues in themselves. Managers' attitudes are shaped by the limiting view that health is a physical disease, and these are not physical issues. Secondly, and even more dangerously, they are often not thought of as issues that seriously affect the workplace.

This attitude is misguided on both counts. These changed and evolving social circumstances can create very real health issues indeed, for as significant sources of pressure they greatly affect the way our employees are able to perform in both the short and the long term. Because of this they are also of huge significance to the employer.

This is clearly demonstrated in the management of absence from work. Time and again employees tell us that family issues are frequently the real cause of their sickness absence, or of their being unproductive at work. But this is rarely if ever 'owned up to'. In many companies the employees feel that this is seen as an unacceptable reason for absence. This says much about the prevailing culture within these organisations, but the real issue is that there is a hidden message that home life should not be allowed to interfere with work life. If it does, and of course it does all the time, then the wise thing for the employee to do is cover it up and invent a more acceptable excuse for the absence.

The shortcomings of this approach should be obvious, for an employee with problems outside of work is not going to be able to stop thinking about them while in the workplace. As we have already said, the whole person comes to work and employers need to be sensitive both to the growing pressures on their employees and their changing support requirements. The visible costs of not acknowledging these needs are significant, as we have already seen, but the hidden costs of lost productivity or lack of involvement are even greater.

Really caring for the wellbeing of the employee means that providing for them while they are in the workplace is no longer enough to ensure their maximum contribution while they are physically at work. There are frequently other pressures coming from factors external to the workplace that will impinge on the ability of the employee even to get to work, let alone function to peak performance while there. Companies interested in getting the most from their employees will need to have a greater appreciation that they have increasingly complex lives outside of the working environment. This will affect their performance and their ability to tackle their occupational pressures.

This focus on the social issues affecting parents should not be taken as a simple plea for employers to invest in on-site child-care facilities or anything so straightforward. Neither is it singling out working women as cases for special treatment. Many lone parents are male and very many more men are actively involved in the care of their children at the end of each working day. Instead it is a plea for employers to understand that the profile of the workforce has changed and consequently so have employee needs. These days a generous company car policy is less likely to benefit a working parent than a clearly demonstrated philosophy towards flexible working when family illness strikes.

Economic Changes

The social framework into which our employees return at the end of each working period has changed, but there are ongoing economic changes that continue to affect both the way we work and the way we feel about work.

Global Competition

A few years ago the Institute of Personnel and Development (IPD) launched a consultative document 'People Make the Difference'. This paper looked at a wide range of economic and social trends that were deemed to have significant implications for organisations in the years to come. Its main argument was that long-term organisational success would require new thinking about people management strategies. New thinking is required, it argued, because of the inexorable growth of global competition in all business activities.

A reduction in international trade barriers and the arrival of new overseas competitors in mature markets have led to a dramatic growth in the number and strength of competitive threats. This has acted as the catalyst for significant changes in the way companies do business. Among these changes are an increasing focus on product customisation and an elevation in minimum standards of customer satisfaction. Exemplary service used to be a point of differentiation, now it is taken for granted. Excellent service has become the norm. Businesses can no longer delight customers by having it; they can only disappoint them and thus encourage them to use a different service provider if they fail to deliver.

People buy things for a variety of reasons, but most customers will decide to purchase according to perceived value based on some combination of price, quality, performance, brand, reputation, service, delivery and support. Increased competition, combined with greater customer expectation, means that companies need to continually improve their performance on each of these criteria. Customers want more for less; they want better quality at a lower price, delivered when they want it and provided by people who are helpful, courteous and responsive. The drive for performance improvement has led organisations to respond with more highly differentiated product and service propositions and to seek ever-faster response times. In order to meet the changing demands of our customers we have metamorphosed our companies from a position where we were inwardly focused, towards a place where we look outwards to respond to what our customers want us to deliver. To stay competitive we look for continuous improvement in all of our business processes, propositions and procedures. We are trying to do all of this with lower costs and fewer resources, and our shareholders want us to do this every year, only more so.

Not surprisingly, all of this means that we have, as the IPD predicted, changed the way we manage our people. No longer do we work in a secure hierarchy, where each employee knows their place in the pecking order, and those who want to can plan their career development. Now we have flat management structures, where decision making is decentralised and devolved down and across the organisation. Project teams and cross-functional working are the norm (a cursory glance at the appointments pages in the Sunday papers will show the demand for project management capabilities). Employees are empowered to take decisions that feel right for them, and to accept responsibility for the outcome of those decisions. Quality, cost efficiency, profitability and productivity are terms that pepper every job description and every quarterly performance review.

To make all of this happen, employees are now expected to be totally focused on the needs of their customers, to demonstrate self-management and commitment and ensure that each makes a personal contribution to the ongoing drive for continuous improvement.

In the modern world of work we demand an enormous amount from our employees and, in the final analysis, we expect them to give freely of *themselves* in order to make all of *our* corporate dreams come true. They cannot possibly do this if they are distressed, ill, preoccupied with problems, or frustrated by the way they are treated.

The Impact of Downsizing

As well as trying to improve every aspect of their products and services, most organisations are engaged in a never-ending drive to reduce costs. Cost reduction affects every aspect of organisational life, from saving a few fractions of a penny on bought-in goods, to relocating a production facility to a country with a lower labour cost. One of the most significant changes in the past decade has been the focus on cost reduction by getting rid of people. Organisations throughout the world have been persuaded that they are carrying passengers, that they have too many layers of management and too many employees. Their response has been to shed staff in unprecedented numbers.

Anorexic Organisations

Many of the organisational changes in recent years have been carried out with the objective of creating a 'leaner' and 'fitter' organisation. These change programmes have concentrated on downsizing, reducing staffing levels, cutting out layers of management and removing people. This is intended to make the organisation cut costs and, in theory, improve efficiency. The problem facing many organisations is that they think that lean and fit are the same thing and, as a consequence, move from being overweight to being anorexic.

The analogy with anorexia is apt. An organisation believes that they've got too many people, that they're overweight and need 'slimming down'. They therefore start shedding staff and, for most of them, find that they are in better shape than they were before. Unfortunately, they don't know when to stop slimming down and they go too far. This is the point where organisations get a distorted view of themselves. They look in the mirror and they believe that they need to lose some more weight, to get rid of more people to remain competitive. Unfortunately, the mirror returns a distorted view. The organisation has already lost all the weight it needs to, it has the right number of people and any further reduction is going to make it weaker, not fitter.

Staffing levels in organisations are about muscle, not fat. Muscles are built through exercise and exertion. Organisational muscles develop when people are stretched and challenged but are damaged when they're stretched too far. It makes sense that a fit, muscular organisation is going to be far more effective than a flabby, overweight one. It will also be more effective than a weak, skinny one. Improving organisational wellbeing is the equivalent of building muscles and improving fitness levels. It's about creating the energy, the stamina and the flexibility to survive in a competitive world. It's not about being indolent or unresponsive and it's not about being weak, tired and lacking in energy.

Changes in Working Hours

Although many organisations gained a great deal of benefit from reducing headcount to an optimal level, the true meaning of 'right sizing', many others cut too far, too deep and too messily. They looked at the financial benefits of saving headcount cost and removed people without really considering the impact on performance or service levels. A huge amount of knowledge and experience was thrown away along with the waste and the people who were left, the survivors, had to try to meet increased performance levels with far fewer resources. The need to do more with less placed an enormous strain on the remaining employees, whose only way of filling the gap was by working longer. Although some of the management gurus who advocated reductions in staffing levels have now changed their view and believe that firms need more people, organisations have adjusted to the new order and are unlikely to ever go back to the staffing levels they enjoyed before the cuts. This means that the demands placed on individual managers and employees are, for most people, greater now than they ever have been. Longer working hours combine with busier social and domestic lives to increase the pressure on staff and reinforce the need for organisations to understand and proactively manage the consequences of extended working.

Working longer hours does not just mean coming in earlier and going home later. With many employees feeling under pressure to meet deadlines and be highly productive, the traditional lunch break has also become a thing of the past. This may not sound significant, but it ably demonstrates how the 'work ethic' is changing.

In March 1997 workplace caterers Eurest sponsored a survey among 1100 employees of UK and Northern Ireland companies, as part of the sixth annual 'Lunchtime Report'. They reported that at the start of 1990s 93% of workers took a proper lunch break; by 1997 this figure had dropped to 44% with 29% of workers claiming they never took a lunch break at all. There are many reasons for this, among them being that for many employees with commitments outside of work, the hour over lunch affords a quality opportunity to complete work that might previously have been done after hours.

There is evidence to suggest that this pattern of work behaviour can easily be detrimental to employee health. An employee who is already stressed can further damage their health by failing to eat properly and snacking at their desk on high fat and high sugar 'convenience' foods. The rapid growth over the last five years, in London at least, in the number of sandwich shops is ample evidence that 'going out to lunch' is a rarity for most. Even where a lunch break is taken, it is likely that the sandwich is taken back to the office and consumed there, and in considerably under one hour! The point is, even where contracted hours stay the same, the pressure is on for greater output and productivity.

Increase in Homeworking

Historically a lack of data has made it difficult to reliably estimate the number of homeworkers. However, in summer 1997 the

Labour Force Survey reported that there were an estimated 1.11 million UK homeworkers, of which some 60% are involved in either clerical and secretarial, associate professional and technical or managerial professions. This equates to about 670 000 people. Many believe that we are at the start of a growth curve similar to that seen in the USA, where the number of homeworkers has trebled from under 4 million in 1990 to over 12 million in 1997. In any event, the figure of 670 000 is up by more than a third from the last figure of 400 000 quoted in a comparable study in autumn 1994.

The concept of homeworking is not new – there has been a tradition for low-paid manual 'out-working' in many European economies for many years. But the accessibility of new technology and changing work practices do seem to suggest that homeworking is an increasingly likely way of working for some.

Like any other form of work, however, it can create its own occupational health issues, some 'traditional' and some new. In 'Home, sweet work: requirements for effective homeworking', Yehuda Baruch and Nigel Nicholson report that homeworkers may well enjoy less work-related stress but they experience a corresponding increase in domestic tension. Six out of ten homeworkers involved in the survey reported that work-related problems were better or much better since they started homeworking, but four out of ten said that domestic stress had worsened. The researchers say that this increase in domestic stress may be the result of respondents' home and work lives becoming blurred and, most interestingly, around half said that their working hours had increased since they started working from home.

Changes in Technology and Information Overload

We live in an age of information overload. For twenty-four hours a day, seven days a week, 365 days a year we are bombarded with information. There is no respite and, for many people, nowhere to hide. Information about work has escaped from the boundaries of the workplace to find people wherever they may be in the world; in the car, on the plane, on the beach, even, in the case of at least one particularly insecure manager, in bed! The drive for 'busyness' and the need to be available to whoever wants us at any time has taken over our lives. We are no longer in control. At the dawn of the technological revolution we were promised a world where the machines would remove the drudgery and we would be free to enjoy a life of leisure. Although most of our homes and offices are packed with labour-saving devices, many of us have less free time than ever.

E-mail

E-mail, in theory, is a wonderful thing. It speeds up communication, removes time barriers, avoids playing telephone tag, enables everyone to share information and facilitates group working. But like all things, only if it's used in moderation. The very ease and speed with which it is now possible to communicate with colleagues and customers means that e-mail can create its own new and particularly potent health issues.

It used to be that when an office worker returned from annual leave, the first day back would be spent opening the post and generally catching up by talking to people. Not so now. Post and conversation may still feature, but the first day back is likely to be spent ploughing through a mountain of e-mail. As fast as it is read and dealt with, the tell-tale 'bleep' is heard and a new one will appear. There is simply no escape from the deluge of information, and e-mail stress is fast becoming a recognised phenomenon.

In its own way e-mail has contributed to a 'hurry up' way of working. The very fact that you can be 'mailed' in an instant means that a considered reply is expected at the same speed. Pressure of work and other demands on the employee's time means that this is not often possible. The reality is that an e-mail arrives, is marked as urgent so it gets read and then sits on the system alongside all the other urgent messages waiting for a reply. In the meantime the phone is ringing, papers are piled on the desk and the desktop computer is waiting for you to finish the spreadsheet or enter the accounts data. Then, in the midst of this information overload, the computer-based diary beeps a reminder that you're late for the next meeting. Is it any wonder that some people feel that all this technology has been created to make sure that there is more work to be done than capacity to do it?

Changes in Employee Expectations

So far we have looked at the way that changes in society, together with changes in organisational structure and climate, have combined to increase the demands on employees. Now we alter the perspective and explore the impact of increased employee expectations on the nature of work.

Just as customers have come to expect more and more from their suppliers, so employees have come to expect more from their employers. In most of the developed economies, just having a job is no longer enough. Employees have come to understand that there is more to work than a simple transaction in which labour is exchanged for money. At the very least, people expect their employers to provide a safe and reasonably pleasant working environment. Above and beyond their basic needs people have a range of expectations that have developed over the years. What people can reasonably expect from work obviously depends on their place in the labour hierarchy. Unskilled labourers in areas of high unemployment may have very limited expectations. People at the top of the labour market, the ones with highly valued skills working in sectors such as the high technology industries where there is a significant shortage of people with the appropriate skills, can expect, and increasingly come to get, almost everything.

Gold Collar Employees

The world at the top of the labour market was described in a *Fortune* magazine feature on the new organisation man. *Fortune* described these young and in demand people as the 'gold collar' workers. With the USA unemployment rate below 5% and more than two-thirds of American adults in the labour force, there aren't enough good people to satisfy employers. Another revealing statistic is that in the USA the unemployment rate for college graduates is below 2% and for people with the right skills, the gold collar workers, there is virtually zero unemployment. According to the Ron Carelli Report in 1996, there were 47 000 vacancies worldwide in the field of computer animation but only 14 000 animators graduated from art school. In the area of management consultancy, firms like Andersen Consulting, or

McKinsey and Co., have an enormous worldwide appetite for the young, able, intelligent individuals they depend on for their business growth. Although the management consultancy firms take a high proportion of business school MBAs, the demand for people with the right skills set and attitude exceeds supply. The 1998 merger of two of the 'big six' professional services firms created PriceWaterhouseCoopers, an organisation with 140 000 staff and a plan to grow massively in the next five years. To do this the firm needs to recruit a great many talented and well-educated individuals. Many of the people it wants to hire will be the same people who other firms are trying to recruit. For people with the relevant skills, it has become a buyers' market.

Although the consulting and high tech firms represent the cutting edge of the desire to be seen as 'the employer of choice', the need is becoming increasingly apparent to many more organisations. Whether the industry sector is pharmaceuticals, engineering, finance or retail, the changing work patterns require more and more work to be done by fewer and fewer people. For businesses to survive in this highly competitive culture where overwork is the norm, they need to protect the health and wellbeing of their employees.

Employee Choice

We now have a situation where organisations are realising that employees increasingly have a choice about who they work for and for how long. This choice is exercised at the time they decide who to work for and is continually exercised during the time they are employed. Any organisation that wants to be able to choose the best possible candidates to fill its vacancies and believes that the quality of its people make a difference to its success, has to realise that it cannot take people for granted. Employers have to get the 'hygiene' factors correct. They must make sure that basic conditions such as pay, holiday entitlement, working environment and so on are attractive and, recognise that, although these conditions are necessary to recruit and retain suitable staff, they will not do so on their own. The motivators, the aspects of work that make a real difference to people who are able to choose, are increasingly to be found in the areas of employee wellbeing. Work isn't only about pay, it's about self-fulfilment. The people that employers most want to attract are those people who understand the nature of choice, the ones that are independent and achievement oriented. These individuals have been brought up in a world where they expect to get what they want. To quote an American guru when asked what these gold collar workers really want, he replied 'They want the remote control'.

The contrast between the way that organisations respond to their customers and the way they respond to their employees is striking. Successful organisations get close to their customers, take the time and trouble to understand their customers' needs and respond to those needs, giving the customers what they want. When it comes to their employees, however, the vast majority of organisations don't listen to their people, don't understand their needs and don't give them what they want. This approach may have worked when people had no choice, when jobs were in short supply and they had to take what they could get. Today's workplace is different; people do have a choice. At its most extreme they can express their dissatisfaction by leaving the organisation and going to work somewhere else. Company loyalty is weaker than brand loyalty and just as consumers show that they will change brands if they don't get what they want, so employees will change companies. Even if people don't leave they show their dissatisfaction by taking time off work, or going through the motions of work without really being involved. Either way the organisation loses.

Bringing the Workplace Together – Optimising Employee and Organisational Expectations

The expectations of the employees to have more and be treated better may, at first sight, appear to be at odds with the expectations of employers that people will work harder, be more committed and do more for less. We argue that these should not be mutually incompatible goals. By focusing on the people, on the whole person, we can work towards a point of optimum wellbeing where the expectations of the employee are aligned with the expectations of the employer (Figure 2.1). Both sides want more. Working in alignment gives them more!

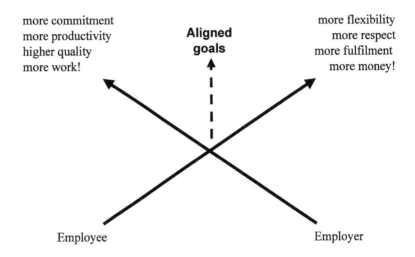

Figure 2.1   *Optimising employer–employee expectations*

THE IMPLICATIONS FOR WORKPLACE WELLBEING

It is obvious that employees are subject to a great deal of change and pressure from forces both internal and external to the workplace. They have much to cope with. Good health is a prerequisite for managing all these conflicting demands and influences, and it is employee wellbeing in the broadest sense which is most likely to suffer because of the complexity and pace of modern life.

Most organisations, as we shall see, invest in employee health up to a point. A good number of them invest quite considerably. But few of them really tackle employee wellbeing in a holistic or global way. With all these changes, and more to come, it seems likely that employers will have to take a more proactive look at the way they deal with employee health.

Funding Wellbeing at Work – Shifting the Burden

Changes in society and in the workplace provide compelling evidence to suggest that employee health deserves investment in its own right. However, even the most sceptical employer may find there are further changes taking place that will make investment in health a necessity. Some of these macro-economic changes already described will probably mean that, in the not too distant future, employers are going to *have* to make more investment in health than they do now.

Hamstrung by falling tax revenues from a shrinking labour force, while at the same time facing increased demand for health care through greater longevity and higher health expectations, there is likely to be a subtle paring back of the amount of available funds for state health care provision. The National Health Service celebrated its fiftieth anniversary in 1998 and among all the special supplements and 'birthday features' there was no shortage of references to the fact that funding mechanisms over the next fifty years will of necessity be quite different to those of the first half century.

In practical terms this means that the burden of care cost is likely to be refocused on those individuals who can afford to pay for it. When this happens, we can expect to see the working population merely transfer this burden onto their employers, in the form of increased demand for health benefits while at work. Employers will therefore be faced with increased health funding cost at a time when most of them will be engaged in rationalising pay and benefits to become ever more competitive.

In a sense this has already happened, with the rapid growth in demand for private health insurance during the late 1980s, demonstrating the employees' ability to 'boost' private provision by demanding specific employee benefits to cover a perceived shortcoming in state provision. This subtle shift of health provision from public to private has been happening for some time. A performance curve for state intervention shows that, relative to the rest of Europe, the UK already has less state intervention in health than some comparable economies.

The UK government's decision in 1994 to remove the employers' ability to claim back statutory sick pay (SSP) for all but the smallest companies was another step in the same direction. The removal of SSP was matched by a corresponding reduction in the employers' National Insurance (NI) contribution, such that if absence levels at the company were 'average' then the company would see a net effect in terms of their cost. However, in an Industrial Society survey carried out that year, companies felt that SSP changes were imposing a significant extra cost, although a third of them were unable to estimate what the extra cost might be. The Industrial Society themselves suggested an estimate of some £1.1 billion annually.

This change in legislation not only contributed several million pounds to the Treasury, but also motivated organisations to try to tackle their sickness absence problems. The theory goes that if an employer can keep absence below the average, then they are gaining more in the reduced employer NI contribution than they are losing through the withdrawal of reclaimed SSP.

It was this change in legislation that fuelled the initial growth in interest about sickness. It is ironic that this should have acted as the catalyst because, even after allowances for NI contribution, the increased SSP cost is still a tiny fraction of what the sickness absences are costing the organisation in other ways. The difference is that the change in legislation made the SSP cost *visible* and therefore measurement has become a necessity. The very invisibility of most of the other real costs of ill health means that in many cases these issues continue unmeasured and unmanaged. Changing legislation and alterations in the way the state funds health care will make many more, previously hidden costs, much more noticeable.

We shall be returning to the notion of visible and hidden health costs in a later chapter. For now the point is that European employers can expect to see an ongoing increase in demand for health investment by their employees, as successive governments subtly change the mix between public and private health care funding. The change in SSP legislation was the first of many UK government initiatives, the most recent being changes to state disability benefits. There are more expected.

SUMMARY

Today's employees operate in a world of work where the pace of change is fast, and the demands made upon their time while at work are great and growing. Outside of work, there is as much change and pressure as there is inside the organisation. Both employee and employer are subject to economic, technological and social factors that impact on their ability to function profitably in all that they do.

As a result the employee's health is potentially under threat and, because of this, so is the company's health. All of this points to a need to change the way we view and manage employee health and wellbeing. The complexity of the factors that influence health, and the scarcity of resources available to manage the outcomes, means that a new approach is required if we are to continue to get the best from our employees and play to win against our global competitors.

3
The True Cost of Employee Ill Health

Growing Awareness of the Costs

The concept of 'good health is good business' is now firmly entrenched in the minds of most human resource professionals. This is to be expected for, as the 'raw materials' of their occupation, one would expect the HR professional to know that health is related to performance, both individually and collectively.

Perhaps more noteworthy is the growing interest in the minds of financial managers of the potential for increased profit through improved health. Let us not forget that these are the people in an organisation who are often thought to be less focused on the 'softer' manpower issues and more on the 'gritty' ones to do with return on investment and profit. Employee health and welfare issues have not traditionally been their concern. The reasons for this developing interest have more to do with cost than welfare. Finance directors like to control costs, and there is now a much clearer appreciation that the organisational cost of employee ill health is very high indeed.

Health of the Nation

It should not be a surprise to find that both parties are now more appreciative of the link between good health and improved business performance. It is after all a commonsensical equation and since 1995, when the UK government's 'Health of the Nation' strategy was launched, there has been no shortage of verbal encouragement for business leaders to take employee health seriously. This increase in noise was coupled with a proliferation in both the quality and quantity of information available to companies about the cost of ill health, as well as freely available guidance on the health promotion tactics they could employ to reduce their exposure.

In setting down their strategy for improving the nation's health, the UK government at that time were quick to see the potential that employers have for making a contribution to changing health behaviour. After all, some 60% of the waking lives of those in employment is spent in the workplace. Articulating the need for and then enlisting the involvement of UK employers was therefore a key plank in the government's health improvement strategy.

The Health & Safety Executive also launched a number of business initiatives, among them the 'Good Health is Good Business' campaign. With extensive press and TV coverage, this campaign was targeted to impress upon business brains that health really does matter and that we can all play a part in improving our nation's health. The incoming Labour government in the UK have also picked up the baton, dropped by the outgoing Conservative administration. The workplace is one of three 'settings for action' isolated in their Green Paper *Our Healthier Nation*. In it they emphasise the key role that employers can play in encouraging and supporting employees to adopt more healthy lifestyles.

Whether driven by promotion from the government of the day or not, employers are now increasingly aware of the growing cost of employee ill health to their business. As a result they are also investing at least a degree of management thinking time in how to deal with the issue of health in the workplace.

This increased health focus is not only in response to a better understanding of the associated costs, but also in recognition of the major changes that are taking place in our society which impact on the workplace. These changes, as mentioned previously, are many and varied, spanning worldwide recession, global health issues such as AIDS and drug use, the growth of technology, changes within family life and population demographics, as well as shifting social policy on health and retirement benefits. But despite recognition of the importance of these factors, cost reduction still remains the single biggest motivator for action on health.

We have already touched on the dimensions of the direct costs associated with sickness absence, as well as some of the other costs associated with ill health such as temporary staff costs, retirement benefits, litigation and so on. But large though they are when combined, these visible costs are still only part of the story. The true cost of employee ill health is considerably greater. Low wellbeing among the workforce, however caused, impacts on the business in very many less obviously measurable ways.

The CBI was among the first to try to quantify the scale of the 'invisible' or indirect costs associated with sickness absence. Estimates have varied from between 60% and 100% of the direct costs attributable to the issue. Given the size of the direct costs of absence in the UK, such a calculation would generate a reasonable figure, but in reality even that is probably dramatically understated. The people are the business. Their efforts on a day-to-day basis turn strategy into reality, profit forecasts into profits posted. Starting from this point of view, it gets easier to see just how many ways employee wellbeing, be it high or low, can affect the business.

In our work with major organisations that have started to try to better understand employee wellbeing, we have come to the conclusion that the hidden costs considerably exceed the visible ones. As it is with the reef, there are far more dangers hidden below the surface of the water than are visible above it.

So where are these hidden costs and can organisations do anything about them?

WHAT ARE THE HIDDEN COSTS?

Staff Turnover

The Cost of Staff Turnover

In presenting a financial case for managing employee wellbeing, it is helpful to estimate the cost of factors such as sickness absence and labour turnover. The MCG Consulting Group carried out an analysis of labour turnover costs. On their calculations, an employee earning £20 000 per annum would cost the company approximately £7500 in direct costs and slightly more again in indirect costs, making a total of £15 500. Incomes Data Services estimate the total cost per leaver at about £15 000. The Institute of Employment studies goes slightly higher and calculates the cost as being a year's salary. MCG illustrate the cost of labour turnover with an example based on a company employing 500 people, with an average labour turnover of 13%. In this organisation, they calculate the cost of replacement to be around £1 000 000 per annum. Reducing labour turnover by just 4% to an annual figure of 9%, arguably a modest target, would save that organisation £300 000 per year. This money of course is pure profit and if the organisation is in a low margin business, could be expressed as several million pounds' worth of sales required to make that profit contribution.

Intellectual Capital

More expensive in the longer term than the considerable short-term costs of recruitment and replacement, is the cost associated with the loss of intellectual capital that occurs when an employee leaves. It may have taken several years of training, development and experience to 'equip' the employee to do their job to the high standard the employer demands. It usually takes a few minutes to walk out of the door. As companies become more and more knowledge based, the losses associated with staff turnover can only get greater.

In building a business case for better health care management it might also be helpful then to assess the true value of employees' intellectual worth, both individually and collectively. Indeed, David Snowden, Director of Knowledge and Differentiation in IBM Global Services, has argued recently that a measure of intellectual capital is needed to act as a market guide to a company's future performance. In his presentation at a CBI/IBM conference in 1997 'The Balance Sheet of the 21st Century Company', he encouraged business leaders to try to quantify their intellectual capital. Placing a value on it, he argues, could act as a guide to the company's future performance where a review of the profit and loss account reflects only the past performance. The quality and stability of the intellectual capital owned by a company can therefore greatly influence ongoing business performance.

As an aside, David Snowden suggests that staff retention could be a useful measure of the company's intellectual capital. If, as seems sensible, stock market analysts were to take notice of employers' attempts to account for their intellectual capital, then reducing labour turnover by better management of employee wellbeing could add quite a considerable sum to the book value of the business as well. In any event, it seems that the true value of intellectual capital is rarely understood. If companies really did appreciate just how much of their current success and future prosperity depend on the capital that they possess now, one would expect to see more evidence that they were proactively protecting it.

Problems in Using Labour Turnover Statistics for Trend Analysis

There are two external factors that need to be recognised when analysing labour turnover statistics. These factors reflect the 'push' and 'pull' of the labour market. 'Push' occurs when people feel dissatisfied with their jobs and start looking around for alternatives but, because there is high unemployment, find it hard to leave until their circumstances become so bad that they are pushed out. This may take a long time and may involve a move to a job with a lower salary or to a less senior role. In this situation, people leave because they really can't take any more and almost anything is better than their current role. In a 'pull' situation, low unemployment means that alternative jobs are easy to find. In these circumstances a dissatisfied employee starts to look around and finds lots of attractive opportunities with other employers. The employee finds that they can change jobs quite easily and are pulled painlessly from one organisation into another.

The pull and push of the labour market makes it difficult to interpret staff turnover figures and compare them over time, or by geography or industry sector. Organisations should recognise that at times of high unemployment people will be reluctant to leave their jobs without another one to go to and finding a job is likely to be quite difficult. When unemployment is low, the labour market is much more fluid. People have greater mobility and may even decide that their chances of finding alternative employment are so high that they can risk leaving without an alternative. Problems within an organisation that would cause people to leave will be masked when other jobs are hard to find. Low levels of labour turnover are not necessarily good indicators of employee wellbeing.

Changes in technology have eroded the role of the unskilled and semi-skilled worker and, to a large extent, the skilled blue collar worker. The pressures have shifted increasingly to customer service, administrative, clerical, technical and managerial employees. This shift in the relative importance of blue and white collar work is reflected in the labour turnover statistics. In the United Kingdom over the past few years, labour turnover rates have steadily declined for blue collar workers and steadily increased for white collar workers. Although the lines have yet to cross on the graph, if present trends continue absence and attendance at work will have shifted from being a shop floor problem to an office floor problem. This trend has a clear impact on the cost of staff turnover. As attrition becomes more of a problem for the more highly paid staff, the cost of finding a replacement and the cost of training that replacement will increase considerably.

Quality

Quality has been a major focus of management attention for many years. Billions of pounds have been spent on quality improvement programmes and most senior management teams regard the quality of their goods or services as a key concern. Although many quality initiatives concentrate on improving processes to eliminate the possibility of error, the importance of the human dimension is acknowledged. There is a clear recognition that people influence quality and their role in quality improvement occurs at several levels. The most obvious is that employees shouldn't make mistakes. The 'right first time' approach has become commonplace. At another level, quality programmes recognise that the people doing the job are those most able to identify and implement opportunities for improvement. Employees are encouraged to work together in groups such as quality circles to spot problems or weaknesses and generate improvement ideas. In many organisations, quality improvement is linked to empowerment and employees are given the responsibility for implementing some of the improvement ideas without having to refer to their bosses.

The attention given to the employees in properly run quality programmes almost inevitably improves wellbeing. Staff feel involved, valued and respected. They are treated as people with ideas who can use their initiative to make measurable improvements in quality. The opposite of this is also true and highlights the impact on quality of a lack of wellbeing.

When employees are not respected, are not involved, or are not supported, it is hard to see why they should have any commitment to quality. Again this works on two levels. People who are worried about their health, concerned about family responsibilities or feel they're under enormous pressure cannot possibly concentrate on the job and so they make mistakes. When people suffer, quality suffers. These mistakes may be errors in doing the job or a lack of care in spotting mistakes. There are many examples of the link between wellbeing and quality and the following story demonstrates the true cost of a quality error.

Geoff worked as a machine setter in a small engineering company in the north of England. His firm made high-value, high-volume products for the business machines industry. The company had invested several years and hundreds of thousands of pounds in trying to win business with a major Japanese manufacturer. They finally won an order and were told that if they performed well further business would follow. Geoff had the job of setting up the machine to make the parts. He was chosen because he was known as a reliable and competent employee. Geoff knew the job was important but he had other, more pressing concerns. His wife had been taken ill and was in hospital, his shift work pattern made it almost impossible for him to look after the children and the family who usually helped out were away. Geoff was worried about his wife and was conscious of the need to get away from work as soon as he could to be with the children. He had set up similar jobs before and, distracted by his domestic worries, did this one on autopilot. He went through the physical motions as usual and the production supervisor keeping an eye on the set up couldn't tell that although Geoff's body was doing the work, his mind was elsewhere. Lack of concentration meant Geoff made a mistake, just a little mistake, but enough to throw out the tolerances on the part. Like many companies with a quality policy Geoff was responsible for checking his own work. Again he did the micrometer measurements without really concentrating and didn't spot the error. He had also taken longer than usual to set the job up, knew he had to get away quickly and cut corners, and he only did one check instead of the three required.

The outcome of this story is that the company produced several thousand parts that were just outside the design specification – they were good but not good enough. Because this was, like many first orders, a rush job and Geoff had been slow in getting the job ready, the parts were shipped without further inspection. They arrived in Japan, went straight to the production line and failed, causing serious loss of production for the customer. The company didn't get a second order.

The consequence of one person's mistake was an enormous loss for his employer. This one minor error led to a loss of revenue from the sale, a loss of future earnings from that customer, a loss of the investment in winning the order, and a loss of reputation for the business. A conservative estimate of the total cost to the company over the next ten years runs into millions of pounds. Of course the company didn't see this as a health or wellbeing issue, they saw it as a systems failure. Their quality processes let the mistake slip through and the investigation into the cause of the error focused on tightening up inspection procedures. They even invested £30 000 in sophisticated electronic equipment to replace the micrometer and improve the accuracy of the measurement. The company, like many others in a similar situation, only considered the visible issues; they didn't look below the surface and ask the obvious question: 'Why would one of our most reliable workers make such a simple error?' If the company had been truly concerned about employee wellbeing, it would have recognised that even the best employees sometimes go through difficult times and spent a few pounds on child care or changed a shift pattern to give Geoff the support he needed during a difficult time.

Creativity and Innovation

Companies cannot stand still and rely on their existing products and services to keep them competitive. The rate of change means that every organisation has to continually improve, invent and innovate if it is to succeed. Even the most revolutionary new products give only a few months' advantage before competitors enter the market. The speed at which businesses in the computer industry develop, market and replace products is an obvious example of the need for a creative and innovative workforce. It's not just the designers and development specialists that need to be creative, it's everyone; from the people on the production line to the accounts clerks. All employees can make a contribution to the intellectual capital of the business and the more they are involved, the greater the leverage the business gets from their collective ideas.

As in the previous examples, the link between creativity and wellbeing works both ways. An organisation with good wellbeing will value and involve its people. People who are involved and valued will be more committed to the success of the business and more willing to contribute. If the company's wellbeing programmes provide support for problems at home and encourage a healthy and balanced lifestyle, employees will be able to give more of themselves to work. Ideas flow more freely from a mind unencumbered with worry.

The negative aspects of a lack of wellbeing also apply. If an employee is worrying about her health or her family, she is unlikely to come up with ideas for new products or services and will not make an effective contribution to continuous improvement groups. She will be at work and will probably do a satisfactory job, but she won't provide that extra spark that takes the company into the next generation of its products.

Few organisations make the link between creativity and wellbeing. The more enlightened ones recognise the contribution that employees can make to business improvement and set up groups and reward schemes to encourage innovation. Only a very few have invested in programmes that appreciate that wellbeing is an essential component of organisational creativity.

The Value of Employee Goodwill Towards the Organisation

Most company assets are listed in the report and accounts. The value to the organisation of their plant and machinery, buildings, raw materials and stock is calculated and accounted for. Depreciation is calculated, along with the return on capital employed and the value of goods and services still in production. More recently, accountants have even started to quantify the value of the brand, and this now also appears in many company accounts as a valuable asset. Rarely if ever does anything appear in the balance sheet for the goodwill of the staff. Although difficult to account for, the goodwill of the employee towards the organisation is enormously valuable. More than that, it can be crucial to the survival of a company when the going gets tough.

Most of the human resource strategies we build now almost assume that this goodwill will be there, although as we have seen there is little strategy in place in many companies to secure the employee wellbeing that must, by necessity, underpin those feelings of goodwill towards the employer.

Employee goodwill is a valuable commodity, for without it most other business strategies will not get past first base. Employees are required now to be willing contributors to the business's success, to give of themselves and to work with energy and creative enthusiasm. This is usually only achievable where there is appropriate recognition of the value of each individual employee's knowledge, experience and commitment to the organisation. As a general rule, employees will maintain a high standard of goodwill towards the company if they feel that they and their contribution are in turn valued by their employer. Yet, in the scramble to stay in front, this softer side of human resource management is increasingly being forgotten.

This is never more evident than during mergers or take-overs, where the immediate focus is on profits and efficiency and a fast turnaround in the company's fortunes. Although a lot is said about them, people issues usually take a back seat and the commitment and passion felt by many employees towards the company is at best taken for granted. At worst, it is not recognised or valued at all. The new management arrive with their own agenda regarding what effective working looks and feels like, heads roll, new blood arrives and those who either choose or manage to stay on often have to subdue their experience and opinions in order not to appear 'old guard'.

What this means for the employees involved is that much of what they believe in, and feel passionate about, must therefore be suppressed. Given that the most motivated of them are often emotionally associated with their work, this means that they finish up having to deny a large part of themselves. Yet we ask them to give of themselves in the pursuit of our corporate objectives, and we continue to demand that they operate with energy and enthusiasm. Many of them continue to do so, but without their earlier conviction and without the drive and passion that they once had. In this situation both parties, the employer and the employee, are the losers.

Often there is a feeling, particularly if company profits were down before the new management arrive, that anyone working in the company at the time when the take-over happens must somehow have been personally responsible for the poor performance. Maintaining the goodwill of the employee in this situation is an impossibility. It is hard to feel benevolent towards an organisation that has just dismissed as 'no longer relevant' the combined experience and knowledge of a large part of the workforce at a single policy stroke.

When this happens to groups of managers, when goodwill is damaged in this way, the long-term effects on the organisation can be far reaching. As with so many other health issues, the effects are not immediately apparent but are hidden 'below the water-line'.

What happens is that the most motivated employees, in the short term, try to get along with the new regime; they try to seem flexible, to show a willingness to change and get behind the new ideas. However, most of the time while they are doing this they will be suppressing their knowledge and opinion on key issues for fear that they are labelled inflexible, unwilling to change and so on. They therefore cannot contribute to the debate on how to implement new strategies and practices. They dare not say that the plans are flawed, even though they may know it because they have been around long enough to see that the approach is wrong. So the plans go ahead anyway. New management believe they are taking the other 'older' managers with them and a jaunty path is set in the wrong direction.

Predictably, stripped in practical terms of their ability to influence and make a difference, these employees do not stay motivated for long and leave. Many of them take their expertise to the competition, where their experience and knowledge is valued at a high price, particularly now that it has been supplemented by a recently acquired knowledge of the new management plans. Sometimes, disillusioned and now lacking confidence in the market value of what they know, they will leave the industry altogether. In any event the new owners have already lost a considerable part of their investment, perhaps the most valuable part. Those employees who leave at the earliest opportunity, or when they can no longer face working in this sterile environment, are the very people who contributed to the company's success. The same success that made the acquisition look like a good business opportunity in the first place. The future commercial results of the 'new' company have already been compromised. Is it surprising that so many mergers fail?

The dangers of the first scenario and the waste in the second should be obvious. Damaging employee goodwill in this way is not just about losing your best 'survivors' to competition though. The reality is worse than that. What happens is that the 'new' organisation is left with the people who stay behind, those who can work in an experience vacuum, who are not sufficiently motivated to care that you do not value their experience. What happens to energy, creativity and enthusiasm then?

It is often for these reasons alone that loss-making companies get turned around into profit-making companies very quickly, only to collapse again as soon as the incoming managers have taken their performance bonuses and moved on. That above-the-line success is bought at a very high price indeed. For in order to strip out all the 'extraneous costs', and push up productivity and profitability to a level where a paper profit is made, the very heart of the business, the people and the goodwill they bear the firm, has had to be ignored. Some good people leave, taking their expertise somewhere else, while other good people remain but are gagged by circumstances into silence, and the 'don't care' brigade stay and do what they are required to do and no more. When this happens the intellectual capital of the business is dramatically marked down.

A little more focus on the broader aspects of employee health would go a long way to prevent this potentially disastrous scenario.

Lower Customer Service Levels

Many service and retail organisations are finding it increasingly difficult to differentiate on the basis of price or proposition alone. For many, the only point of differentiation between them and their increasingly global competitors is customer service. But one of the major implications of poor employee health is reduced customer service.

Employees who are below par, either physically or mentally, do not give of their best in front of your customers. This is because they are either absent from work and therefore completely unable to exercise the customer care skills you have invested thousands in giving them, or they are present but not at their best. Chronic back pain, coupled with several successive 'difficult' customers, is unlikely to produce a successful interaction between the employee and the customer. It follows that if their health is improved, day-to-day customer satisfaction will be easier to predict too.

Adequate customer service is no longer sufficient. In an increasingly competitive world we expect our employees to *delight* our customers. Dealing with our company needs to be not just effective but uplifting. It is never acceptable to say to a disgruntled customer, 'I would help you but I do not feel very well. Could you ask one of my colleagues?' No one does this. All of our customer care programmes are based on the assumption that as an employee we accept that we represent our whole organisation every time we interface with a client or supplier. We are therefore encouraged to subdue our anger, pain, irritation, fatigue, frustration and any other 'negative' emotions, in order to impress customers with our concern and attention to their wants and desires. This has become a prerequisite and we demand it of all the business contacts that we make.

Our employees are asked to 'go the extra mile' to deliver exemplary service, regardless of what happened to them on the way to work this morning, during work this morning or maybe might happen to them when they get home this evening. Most of them manage to do it, all of the time. Many of them do it without much in the way of support from their employer. Sometimes though it may not be possible and then the cost is great.

'For want of a nail the battle was lost', so goes the fable. The ultimate cost of reduced customer service is fewer customers. More appreciation of the pressures that employees might be quietly dealing with while they are delighting our customers could well make all the difference. If that appreciation were turned into the provision of more flexible working practices, proactive health and sickness management and support systems to help them deal with those pressures, then the battle may not be lost at all.

A major airline implemented an employee assistance programme for all their cabin staff on the basis of just this type of thinking. Unique occupational pressures associated with travelling to different countries and in different time zones mean that cabin staff can have very real difficulties dealing with problems originating either inside or outside of work. Employees might board a plane at 5.00 am and not complete the round trip until three days later. A worrying problem occurring that morning is therefore going to be unresolved and, more importantly, stay that way for at least 72 hours. Yet during a great part of that time they are going to be involved in physically demanding work that requires them to be cheerful, polite, empathetic, sensitive and responsive to their passengers. The airline recognised that this was both a tall order and a dangerous risk.

The introduction of an employee assistance programme meant that the cabin staff would have access to help and advice 24 hours a day, accessible anywhere in the world. The cost was deemed to be worth it, so valuable is the reputation for exemplary service aboard its aeroplanes.

SUMMARY

The real cost of ill health is likely to be far greater than most employers can imagine. Business plans depend on the full co-operation and involvement of everyone in the organisation. If ill health means that they are absent from work, or are present but not functioning to full capacity, they will not be delighting our customers, building competition-beating marketing plans or making the best products on the market. If people are not working effectively, they are costing the business money. It is very hard to estimate the total cost of poor employee wellbeing, but even a superficial calculation of the true cost of the various factors, such as poor quality, poor customer service, lack of innovation and low productivity, will add up to a figure that represents a significant cost to the business. It may be 10% or 30% of turnover or 20% or 50% of pre-tax profits. Whatever the figure, it will certainly be many times higher than the traditional estimate of the cost of health calculated on the cost of sickness absence.

4

Building a Strategy for Health

We have seen that our employees' health is potentially at risk, and that the true cost of ill health is far in excess of the visible cost. So, what do we do about it? As employers, do we have to accept that people get ill and it's the responsibility of employees to keep themselves well enough to get to work, or is there a better way? The simple answer is 'yes'; there is a better way. It is obvious that employees ultimately have to accept responsibility for their own health, but this does not mean that the employer does not have roles and responsibilities towards helping them to stay in good health and supporting them when they are ill. It is not necessary to let corporate ill health 'just happen'. Organisations can influence health and wellbeing and are able to change events and outcomes.

In short you can actively *manage* health and wellbeing. More than this, you can and should build a strategy for health, with mission, objectives and goals, in much the same way as you would develop a strategy for any other major business ambition. Theory and practice do not converge, however. Most organisations have strategy development for all their major business areas, but not for health. Arguably, however, a strategy for employee health should be of the highest priority, for none of the other business objectives can be fully realised without the effort and commitment of the workforce themselves.

WHAT IS A STRATEGY FOR HEALTH?

Frequently, when the word strategy is mentioned, people start to look uncomfortable. There is a feeling that adopting a strategic approach to anything will involve layers of difficulty and probably expense. This can happen, but in this context a strategy for health does not mean expensive or difficult. Put simply, it means that you should have a plan for employee health, just as you will have one or more sales plans, marketing plans and so on. You should have analysed where you are now in terms of the real health issues faced by your employees. You should have a clear idea of where you want to get to with employee wellbeing; which ill health costs you want to reduce and by how much. You should then develop a vision and road map for how you want to get there. In other words bring to bear the basic rules of strategic thinking:

- Where are we now?
- Where do we want to be?
- How do we get there?

This approach is not complicated, but it does require the organisation to commit to viewing employee health holistically. The company must recognise that there is a need to properly align health investment with *real* employee health needs and not *perceived* ones. Achieving the correct alignment will involve some change and possibly investment, in order to gain a more robust understanding of what the real health risks are. This may mean an investment in time, or perhaps the application of some formal measurement techniques. But essentially the approach remains a simple one.

Modern Myths about Health Care Management

Health is too Big to Manage

Organisations with a strategic approach to managing health have had to make one enormous leap forward before they could even start to deal with the issues. They have had to overcome the first obstacle, the familiar idea that health is too big to tackle.

Progress with the holistic approach to corporate health management has been hampered by the view that the issue is just too big and unwieldy. There is a belief that there are so many stakeholders that it would be inappropriate to give any one group of personnel responsibility for managing health. So, invariably, the issue is broken up and the various pieces distributed across the organisation. As we shall see, one of the results from this is a fragmented approach to the real issues embodied by a long string of health interventions that do not come together to meet any specified objectives.

Health can't be Measured

The other belief is that employee health cannot be tackled because in totality it is immeasurable. The dimensions of the issue and the different manifestations of health and ill health are so varied that it cannot be quantified. Since nobody wants to assume ownership for something that cannot be measured, this provides a ready-made excuse for inactivity, or a little tweaking on the edges such as the introduction of health screening for senior executives or an employee assistance programme.

Thus for many, employee health management remains a concept safely out of reach and stays, as was once confessed by a senior HR professional, 'right over there in the difficult box'. No one dare take the lid off in case it cannot be jammed back on before the 'beast' gets out.

This fear is particularly noticeable when it comes to mobilising organisations to investigate the prevalence of issues like occupational stress. Often there is a sense that if the company makes a move to measure or find out more about the issue, then they will have 'admitted' that there is a problem. By default they will then have committed themselves to finding a solution, and so it is best to leave well alone. You do not have to manage what you have not measured. This is the same principle that the ostrich works on, of course; if I cannot see you, you cannot see me. If we do not know how big some of these health issues are, we will not have to do anything about them. With luck they will just go away!

In the UK at least, the legislative environment with regard to the necessity for risk assessment is changing. Most HR professionals and industry commentators expect the EU Health & Safety Requirements to be more proscriptive than we have become used to. This may eventually force an end to the fear of measurement.

Statutory requirement or not, employee health can easily be measured, on a number of indices. Often it is not even necessary to involve the employees directly. You just have to know what to look for.

Why Do We Need a Strategy for Health?

The main issue, as we have seen in the preceding chapters, is cost in all its manifestations. The costs are there, whether you measure them or not. But in recent years more companies have started to try to count the cost of ill health for themselves and to calculate it in terms that are relevant for them. In doing so they have found that inaction carries too high a price – even measured against the 'traditional' indices of sick pay, ill health retirement costs and other direct costs.

But there are other major reasons for taking action on the issues. Some of them are not about cost reduction, but about positive health gain.

Competitive Advantage

Tighter manpower budgets mean that the number of people available to carry out the work required is lower than was once the case. More than ever, cost efficiency and productivity are the objectives for most modern business managers. All companies are looking to achieve maximum output from their teams, be they sales, manufacturing or customer service. To achieve this, many thousands of pounds are spent in training and development for each employee. Many more management hours are spent examining new ways to achieve organisational efficiency, through the adoption of more sophisticated technology and clearer working practices. But none of this is effective if employees are not fit and present for work. As much thinking needs to go into ensuring employees are in possession of high wellbeing while at work, as planning how to maximise their contribution through good management practice and reorganisation.

If they are absent, then they are not making any contribution at all. If they are either physically or mentally unwell, then they will be making less than their optimal contribution. Moreover as we have already seen, the 'unwell employee', however defined, is potentially a danger to the company. Not just because of the increased potential for accidents, although this is hazard enough, but because of the increased potential for 'intellectual accident'. Poor decision making brought on by physical discomfort, social and domestic distress or just low levels of mental wellbeing generally could have damaging consequences at all levels. The enormous damage that one individual can do to a business's competitive advantage was illustrated in the example of the cost of quality described in Chapter 3.

In an environment where customer service is all, the employee who is motivated, well supported and frankly passionate about his organisation can make a contribution to the organisation's success that is disproportionate to the amount of real cash investment in him. In one case study example, the smaller of two competing companies confessed that their sales people found it extremely difficult to sell against the team from the larger company. This was not because of superiority in brand, product or price. It was, the contact said, that when these sales people were in the room it was like 'being in the company of a deeply religious person'. The commitment and enthusiasm that these employees had both for both their proposition and the company they work for was so profound it was almost tangible. It was clear that the customers could feel it and were enthused by it. As a result it was almost impossible for the other company to unseat existing business or beat them to new business. He concluded by saying: 'I do not know how you do it (to your staff) but it certainly works.'

When we deal with an organisation as customers, we are actually only making contact with the people in it. It is a cliché but your employees *are* the organisation. They are the face of the company, and the arms and the legs. Organisations don't look after customers, people do. When we accept the prime importance of people, it's easy to see how healthy employees can build real competitive advantage.

Maximising Return on Investing in People

Keeping employees at work and securing their maximum contribution while at work is a fast route to increasing overall productivity. Arguably, after capitalising on the technological revolution, reduction in industrial disputes and adoption of the latest thinking in organisational effectiveness, employee health management affords the last great opportunity for productivity enhancement by reducing the average amount of 'downtime' in all its manifestations. The significant variation that exists between the performance of different organisations is not purely down to the way in which work is organised. Employee attitudes and the way people are managed are as big a determinant of productivity as so-called 'organisational effectiveness'. The role that employee wellbeing and health management can play in this should be obvious.

From a Cost Centre to a Profit Centre

By promulgating and then overseeing the adoption of a health care management strategy the human resource or occupational health professional can change the way they are seen by the organisation. They can place themselves and their department in a position where they are able to demonstrate a measurable contribution to the organisation's success. Many of the managers responsible for the 'people' side of the enterprise have said that frequently they and their departments struggle to be seen as contributors to the business. Instead many feel that they are seen as a drain on the company's resources, always 'taking out' rather than 'putting in'.

By adopting a strategic approach to managing wellbeing, this view can change, as the benefits of health expenditure and employee wellbeing become more measurable through increased attendance and productivity and reduced downtime. This is all part of changing the focus of health, away from soft 'welfare' issues into hard commercial realities. It is easier and often more appropriate in this case to start by focusing on the visible health and wellbeing issues of attendance and attrition. Improvements in these areas are usually easier to measure and will demonstrate the benefit of proactive intervention. Hopefully this will provide the platform from which to launch other initiatives designed to reveal and manage the hidden wellbeing issues.

Business Plans and Health Plans

We believe that employee wellbeing is a critical component of organisational success and, as such, is an integral part of business planning. Organisational strategic planning must include clear strategies for health. Business plans should show how the people issues are aligned with business objectives, and budgets for developing wellbeing should be built into the financial plans. In far too many organisations the wellbeing issues are either ignored or treated as an afterthought, with the inevitable consequence that nothing gets done because 'it wasn't in the budget'. Likewise, when health features in the plans at the macro level, then it follows that it should also feature in local management objectives. The development of real health measures and including them as key performance indicators for managers would go a long way towards building shared responsibility for the issues.

How Many Companies Have a Formal Strategy for Managing Health?

In our work with companies we have found that the answer to this question is 'very few'. Most organisations we speak to do not have any overall direction or policy regarding health care management. Plenty of health investments are made, but these are purchased ad hoc and often survive from year to year because they are difficult to remove from the benefits package. Decisions regarding the type of health investment to make are usually made in isolation, by individuals in separate departments. It is very rare for these purchases to be made as part of a strategy for health improvement with specified goals and key performance indicators. Sometimes a strategy for health can be found at the vision stage, but often this has not evolved into an integrated range of health care services geared towards meeting the stated objective.

The situation is changing. Perhaps largely because of the

exposure given to the cost of sickness absence by the CBI and others, there has been a noticeable growth in the number of companies looking at the concept. Some of them are trying to get more organised in health, others are starting to appreciate that the issues may need tackling in a less tactical way. However, the number of companies who have really 'grasped the nettle' and adopted a strategic approach is still quite small.

Focus on Reducing the Cost of Illness

It is ironic that workplace health management has traditionally been focused on illness or, more specifically, on taking out insurance cover to limit exposure to the costs. For most companies, the primary focus of health at work has had little to do with improving the wellbeing of the workforce. Organisations think they are doing a good job if they are able to reduce the cost of their health insurance premiums, the cost of sickness absence, the number of ill health retirements and so on.

There has been growing interest over the past few years in the concept of integrated health management. While there appears to be no common definition for what this means, the most frequently cited models now turn around the idea that if employee health data is integrated, this can facilitate early identification of the cases that are going to cost the most money. Once identified, the theory goes, the cases can be proactively managed and the cost reduced by returning the employee to work faster, mitigating the employer liability claim and so on. There are significant positives in this approach, among them the possibility for providing support to employees while they are unwell (even if the motive is just damage limitation), but using the concept of integration in this way misses the point. Rarely, it seems, is the approach extended (in line with the original concept) to the potential for using integrated health information to identify *potential* risks and take primary preventive action. Most of the focus is towards managing ill health outcomes to lessen the financial impact on the business.

There is little recognition that many of these ill health episodes and attendant costs, which the companies adopting this approach are now feverishly case managing, may actually have been caused by the employer in the first place.

The reason for the emphasis on cost reduction is that the results are measurable and fairly simple to identify. It is relatively easy to establish a benchmark for long-term sickness absence and agree a target reduction in total number of days lost or percentage reduction in absence rate.

Organisations manage what they can measure. Because there is little understanding of the benefits of the healthy workplace, they fail to focus on the positives and instead concentrate on reducing the negatives. This is analogous to running a business by focusing exclusively on cost reduction. The business may get some benefit and the people involved in this process can take pride in having reduced overheads by 7%, stock levels by 10%, cost of manufacture by 15%, etc. The problems arise when this concentration on cost reduction means that the business fails to pay attention to sales, quality, customer service, and all the other things that are essential for business success. It isn't enough to be the lowest cost provider; there may be some short-term benefit in this approach but the business is simply not sustainable. It's the same with employee health. If the only concern is reducing the cost of illness, the picture is distorted and opportunities are missed. Cost reduction does not lead to a more effective workforce.

Managed Care

The growth of managed care in the UK private medical insurance market and, in particular, the popularity of third-party administrators in the late 1980s early 1990s are clear signs that many organisations have focused on cost reduction. Faced with rapidly increasing premiums, employers have sought to obtain treatment for their employees at lower cost, rather than seek to reduce the cost by lowering the number of times their employees need treatment.

This does not mean that organisations have not tried to influence the number of times an employee uses the insurance. Many major corporate plans now contain Excess and Co-insurance clauses. These require the employee to make a contribution to the cost of their treatment and so have a restraining effect on the number and value of claims made. This clearly has an impact on claims experience, but does not add much to the process of health management. Indeed, critics argue that this merely forces the 'less well off' employee back onto the NHS waiting list, where their condition deteriorates further and their symptoms continue to keep them from work on a regular basis.

Such cost containment techniques work well in doing just that, restraining costs, but they are not addressing the underlying cost driver – the employee's health risk and ill health reality. Managing the cost of treatment is an important part of providing health benefits. Employers are right therefore to work with their insurers and advisers towards securing the most appropriate treatment for their employees, at the most appropriate price. But it is only managing the care. The next wave of cost reduction in medical insurance premiums can only really come from reducing the number of people coming forward for treatment. This means managing the health and not the cost.

Some employers are aware of this issue, and here there is recognition that a change of focus is required. These companies are working less on negotiating down the cost of insurance cover for treatment each year, and are asking more questions concerning what their health partners can offer in risk assessment, health maintenance and ill health prevention, rather than just care management.

But at the current time these employers are few and far between. The majority of those who are buying into health insurance cover are still feverishly working on more and more complicated administrative arrangements with their insurers. The motivation for this is still geared towards reducing the cost of treatment, rather than building strategies to reducing the demand for treatment, through improving employee health.

What Happens if You Approach Health Care Management Without a Strategy?

Unable to Calculate Health Benefits

Perhaps one of the reasons why company health care has traditionally been seen as a welfare issue rather than a commercial one lies in the way health care has been managed in our economies. Until the health care reforms introduced by the last Conservative government, the provision of health care in the UK had been predominantly unfettered by the traditional free market principles of supply and demand. For many, the view is that this has led to a disregard for questions of efficiency and maximisation of the resources employed. Whether this view is correct or not, the point is that this is likely to have affected the way we regard the allocation of our company's resources in health.

A senior occupational health practitioner in a large blue chip company was once asked how she had succeeding in obtaining an increase in her health care budget of some 10%. She had achieved this at a time when the UK was in the grip of recession and all budget holders were being asked to 'sharpen their pencils' for the coming year. She was asked the question because it was interesting to know how she had managed to prove the return on the previous year's investment. Few occupational health practitioners are able to do this and so it seemed probable that she had demonstrated a return of some magnitude in order to secure the same, let alone more, funds for health in the coming year. She gleefully announced that it had not been necessary (presumably she said 'trust me I am a doctor'!). The budget was uplifted, as she said the Board were keen to continue investing in their employees' health because 'they knew it was doing them good', even though they could not prove it.

This is a fine tribute to the company concerned, in that it was clearly willing to continue investment in this important issue. But it is worrying too. As our organisations become tighter and more focused on economic return, it seems unlikely that this type of scenario will repeat itself very often. In time, occupational health practitioners like this one will be called to account for the money that is spent in terms of identifiable return on investment. The concern is that when they are, they will not be able to demonstrate the health gains that have been made, or be able to do so in terms that convince their executives and shareholders. When the going gets tough, few companies will continue investing beyond the bare minimum required to stay within health and safety legislative requirements, if they cannot see a valuable return. There are simply too many other ways to spend the money.

One of the reasons that occupational health spending has

stayed on or around £130 million in the UK is probably because occupational health professionals, and all others making health care investments on behalf of their company, have not been able to quantify the benefit their investments have conferred on their companies. This is not because they lack the accounting skills, but because much of what they are trying to achieve does not integrate into an overall health strategy for the company, if such a strategy exists at all.

As a result they are rarely able to demonstrate positive health gains because there was no clear picture of where they started. All that happens is that when the supplier contract comes up for renewal there is a lot of discussion about price, the benefit being assumed to be incalculable, and more debate about whether we can 'do without it' this year. Invariably the stakeholder manager defends the corner and the health investment survives in the benefits package for another year. But now the hunt is on for a cheaper supplier or a better deal. Value is measured in terms of price relative to competitors, rather than the overall effectiveness of what is being offered.

Health Care Purchasing is Fragmented

What has been most notable while researching this book, and also in day-to-day liaison with human resource and occupational health professionals, is that there is no shortage of money being spent on health in many UK companies today. Good health is good business for health care suppliers too, and a considerable amount is expended in many companies in the name of health investment. What is happening though is, due to the lack of strategy built into the management of employee wellbeing, health spending is invariably focused on the *sickness* episode rather than health improvement.

Put another way, the health spending is aimed at dealing with ill health rather than promoting good health. In effect, companies are often waiting for ill health or the ultimate manifestation of ill health, death itself, to strike, and then either insure against the cost or proffer a solution to modify the impact. To illustrate this point, there follows a list of health spending in one particular company. This information was provided in answer to the question 'What health costs do you have?

- Private Medical Insurance.
- Insurance Premium Tax.
- Permanent Health Insurance/Critical Illness Cover.
- Disability Insurance.
- Eye Tests.
- First Aid.
- Sick Pay.
- Employee Counselling.
- Company Doctor.
- Occupational Health Referrals.
- Compensation Claims.
- Employee Litigation.
- Ill Health Retirements.

The list shows considerable investment in health issues with nearly all the focus on repairing ill health rather than maintaining good health.

One of the related problems is that in any company there will be several people, even several departments, who are making health care investments. The purchase of the health insurance will be one person's responsibility, the purchase of employee liability insurance another. Health screening is purchased by one person, occupational health services by somebody else.

The point is that there is rarely one clearly defined group, or person, who has responsibility for health as a 'global' issue. As before, even organisations that have an occupational health function tend to view this as having responsibility for health and safety issues. They do not generally have responsibility for other health care purchasing decisions and in most cases are not consulted by their colleagues who do make these investment decisions. As we have said before, the traditional view is often that occupational health is concerned only with the effects of work on health. Very rarely does it seem that anyone in the company is tasked with focusing on the much broader effects of health on work.

It is therefore almost inevitable that individual health care purchase decisions are often made in isolation. Where there is a degree of consultation with other functions within the business this is more often to discuss issues such as price and eligibility, than the fit of the intended purchase with any overall business plan for employee health management.

There are clear reasons for this. Health does, after all, affect every department one way or another and so in theory all parties could have a view on where the health investment should be placed. Each manager can visualise their own personal, managerial or departmental benefits for the introduction of say an employee assistance programme, subsidised gym membership, smoking cessation programme, stress management workshop and so on. Each person tasked with a health care purchase, functionally aligned within their organisation, will be keen to 'fix' their bit of the 'jigsaw'. As they do this, the more altruistic among them will also be visualising the benefits that will be coincidentally conferred by their purchase on other areas of the business. The purchase looks sound − there are 'lots of reasons for doing this'. The problem is that rarely have the reasons been aligned to specific and prioritised health care issues. As a result no one manager has a clear view of what the completed jigsaw picture is supposed to look like.

Many health care purchases are still highly emotive. Perhaps this is because the traditional impetus for the introduction of private medical insurance and other benefits like employee assistance programmes have come from human resource departments. These are the departments who are most in tune with the human aspects of the company's day-to-day activities. They want them in the benefits package because other companies have them and because they believe it will make the employees feel better about them as employers. Each individual buyer sees and feels these benefits differently and so develops their own reasons for wanting the health benefit to be part of what they offer in the recruitment market.

What this says though is that health care investments are often made as employee benefits, with the wish to build a strong and competitive recruitment package as the primary motivator. They may accidentally confer some benefit on the organisation, but this is rarely calculated formally at the outset. In these times of leaner budgets, most do have to make some attempt at proving the business case in order to wrestle the cash from the finance director, but these are usually more qualitative than quantitative.

Because of the 'emotional' nature of their purchase and because of the number of personnel involved in making these decisions, the health benefits themselves are not necessarily linked in any cohesive way either. Screening, occupational health services, fitness club memberships, employee counselling and information services, crèche and child care facilities and so on are often made available to different groups of employees, without any evident plan for how they fit together to maximise benefit to both the employee and the employer. In any event it is unlikely that they would fall together as a cohesive strategy because each person involved in the buying process has a different organisational driver. Some decisions are made by finance and some by personnel and what they expect the gains to be are usually wildly different.

Clearly, all of this has repercussions for the effectiveness of health expenditure and it most certainly reduces the ability of any manager making a health investment to calculate the return on the money spent.

Changing the Role of Occupational Health

As we have said many times already, it is not that UK companies are ignorant about the importance of health. Health awareness is not new. Most companies who can afford it have some health benefits available for their employees, either paid for or sponsored. Some of the larger ones also have formal occupational health provision, although a survey conducted by the Employment Medical Advisory Service (EMAS) a few years ago revealed that some 85% of UK companies have no formal occupational health provision, either in-house or subcontracted.

Much of this is to do with the fact that legislation often provides the major impetus for health spending. In the UK, health and safely legislation is generally permissive rather than prescriptive. This is in contrast with other European countries such as Germany, where employers are required to carry out more specific health surveillance and maintenance procedures. Even where formal occupational health provision is made within UK companies, the focus of attention is more towards the *safety* aspects than health, with a 'business' goal to stay quietly within the legislative guidelines but go no further.

Those organisations that have occupational health provision have seen their focus of attention change. Many of the occupational health issues typically associated with heavy industry have declined in prevalence, legislation driving more effective risk assessment and health surveillance. But as they have declined, new occupational health issues, such as work-related upper limb disorder and stress, have risen to prominence. Nearly always though, the focus still seems to be on 'loss reduction' rather than on positive health gain.

This approach has significant implications for expanding the role of occupational health. The term occupational health usually brings to mind a dispensary service, led and administered by specialist doctors and nurses, all of whom are well versed in current health and safety legislation and who are acutely sensitive to all industrial and commercial irritants. They are expert physicians but many lack the business and management skills required to demonstrate the benefits of employee wellbeing to their more cynical colleagues. Unfortunately, other functional areas of the organisation have typically seen many occupational health departments as somewhat peripheral to the main business activity of the firm. As a result they have often suffered from under-investment, both in terms of funds available and input to organisational planning activities.

It is of course vital that they focus attention on the potential for an employee's health to be affected by the work that he or she does. We believe, however, that it is just as important to focus on the extent to which employees' health may affect the way they work and the effect this has on organisational success. Any consideration of occupational health should take into account both views. The more forward-thinking occupational health professionals recognise the value of their role in influencing organisational policy. They appreciate the need to be a key part of the leadership team, advising the Board to promote wellbeing and assess the human (health) cost of each major planning decision. Occupational health professionals should be at the forefront of the campaign to help their organisations understand the commercial benefits of a healthy workforce and work with their colleagues to develop effective strategies for improving wellbeing at work. Unfortunately it does not always work that way.

Leadership and Management of Health

It is important to differentiate between leading on health issues and managing sickness. The distinction is important. Leadership is about doing the right things. Managing is about doing things right. At the moment, a few organisations are managing ill health; they've developed good measurement tools, a better understanding of the cost base and, on the whole, manage ill health well. However, are they doing the right things? It's about shifting the emphasis, about looking again at the whole issue of *health* at work and re-evaluating the things that organisations do. We may be doing things right, but are they the right things to do?

Doing the right things means that your interventions will be correctly targeted, which has obvious financial benefits in terms of increased payback. There are improved human benefits too, in that employee attitudes towards the investment will be more positive because of the increased likelihood of what Adam Smith would have called 'enlightened self-interest' in what is being offered. If the benefit looks to be of use to you, then you are more likely to value it. The right interventions must therefore be targeted at the right people at the right time.

If a detailed investigation is carried out into what the real needs are, then most interestingly the interventions that need to follow are rarely what were first thought. Thankfully, often what is needed is not gym membership for all, but something far less expensive and much more specific. Companies who have taken the plunge and audited for stress among their workforce have found that the solutions were not what they had feared. If interventions are appropriately targeted to real risks, then solving the problem may be far cheaper and will have greater benefits for the organisation. Stress auditing is a good example to use, as very often the solutions are business improvements such as process or job redesign, rather than reducing workload by increasing staff numbers.

The 'low cost–better productivity' solution is illustrated by the results of a stress audit conducted for a company in the communications industry. The results showed that the vast majority of employees reported low pressure from the amount of work they had to do and little sense of achievement. Many of them also reported that they felt only about 80% of their time was productive. Other results from the audit showed that the employees felt they lacked influence and had little control over their work. The audit highlighted a key problem in the organisation: people were not being challenged. They were constrained by over-bureaucratic processes, not involved in their work, and needed more not less stimulus. In other words they were bored and frustrated. The solution was to create more challenge for the employees, to find ways of decentralising power and giving greater responsibility to people. Far from adding to the costs, the interventions were designed to increase productivity and gain more benefit from the individual abilities of staff at all levels.

SUMMARY

As with any other piece of strategy development, the core process is planning. If we were planning a competitive strategy we would concentrate on new directions for growth rather than cost savings and operational efficiencies. We would concentrate on top line rather than bottom line improvement. In the broader sense, building a competitive strategy is not about next year's budget or operating plan. Rather it is a team-based approach that focuses on building competitive advantage in the market place by developing and implementing strategies that build the business. It absolutely requires the involvement and commitment of senior managers and the commitment of the whole organisation to its implementation.

All of this holds true for the development and implementation of a health care strategy. There is a real need to understand the health profile of your employees better, in order to set the plans for improvement, implement them and then measure your successes. You need to set goals and objectives and, in order to have a goal, you have to have a better understanding of your starting point. The mission, goals and objectives require the commitment of the whole organisation and, in particular, the unequivocal support of senior management. In many organisations, changes in the strategies for health will only produce the desired benefits when combined with a fundamental shift in organisational culture.

5
Organisational Health Dynamics

THE NEED FOR MEASUREMENT

It is an old saying but it is true; it's hard to manage what you can't measure. As we have already seen, a reluctance to identify the health issues faced by employees and quantify the effects of poor wellbeing on the organisation has meant that, in most cases, health is not being managed. It follows that any attempt to develop a strategic approach to improving wellbeing must start with the measurement and analysis of the issues.

Organisations that want to improve wellbeing at work will need to invest in gaining this clearer understanding. They will also need to measure these issues in ways that provide a benchmark against which they can assess progress. They need to put a stake in the ground so that they can see how far they have moved – it's very hard to demonstrate progress if you don't know where you started. This investment need not be expensive but will require time. Time to search out all the available data that may be relevant to health and wellbeing issues and time to scrutinise the information cross-functionally to uncover what it is telling you about current, emergent and future employee health issues.

In addition to the relatively straightforward measurement of existing health data you will need to spend time and devote resources to finding out more about some of the less easily measured aspects of wellbeing – the hidden costs of ill health. These may include issues such as stress at work, underlying physical health problems, employee lifestyle behaviours and levels of morale and motivation. The good news is that this investment will be repaid many times over by the increased effectiveness that comes from health interventions targeted at the right employees. Most organisations have little understanding of the reality of corporate ill health and, as a consequence, spend money in the wrong areas. For these businesses the investment they make in gaining a better understanding of the real health profile of their company enables them to redirect existing resources to greater effect. They do not necessarily need to increase the amount they spend on health. The process is simple and straightforward. Understanding 'where are we now' will greatly clarify 'where we want to be' and 'how do we get there'.

Adopting a strategic approach to employee wellbeing does not therefore necessarily mean extra investment. However, a concerted effort to measure even the most visible manifestations of employee ill health, from short-term sickness absences through to ill health retirements, should provide more than enough evidence to build the business case for investment in workplace wellbeing.

What Data Can We Use?

Getting to grips with the health dynamics of your organisation means starting to break down some of the bigger issues and measure both their prevalence and their effects. But what should you measure? In the long run we need to look beyond the obvious if we want to know what is really going on. However, in an environment where very little investigation has been carried out at all, the first place to *start* is with the obvious, the most visible health and wellbeing issues of sickness absence and staff turnover. An important point to note is that, as a general rule, companies already possess more data than they realise about the health of their employees. They may not be using the data to its fullest extent, they may not even have thought to look at it, but usually there is some data around that will give a first-line indication of the key issues. Sickness absence data, even if poorly recorded, can provide some indication of health issues, as can an analysis of staff turnover. Information concerning the incidence and treatment patterns of employees and their dependants making use of company health insurance is also valuable. Data is usually available from providers of employee counselling services on the range and frequency of usage by employees, and health information can often be collated without breaching employee confidentiality from health screening programmes that may be in place. Company doctors make reports, as do the doctors and nurses who carry out occupational health referrals. Then there is information collected on ill health retirements, employee liability claims, workplace accidents and litigation. Still more information can be found in employee opinion surveys. Top-line information on the visible issues is all around if you know where to look.

Unfortunately, unless a strategic approach to wellbeing has been adopted in the past, the available data sets are unlikely to fit together particularly neatly and, with the possible exception of sickness absence data, some of these data sets are not particularly helpful in isolation. They are all important pieces of a jigsaw but, metaphorically, they will be from different boxes. Health insurance claims data can be manipulated to provide good information but only on the employees that are covered by it. Health screening data is another useful source of information, but again the employees who take up the option of a health screen may not be the same people who have claimed on the health insurance policy. Sickness absence data can vary enormously, in both quantity and quality, but at least it should give the widest coverage of employees. The problem here is that you may have records of the incidence of time off but no information on why the time was taken. This makes it difficult to link with data from other sources. In the same way, staff turnover data will give you an accurate picture of how many people have left, but may provide very little information on why they left or the key issues that prompted their search for alternative employment.

As we will see, the ability to link your health data is important, and although unlinked data can be difficult to work with, it is better than nothing. Even if the data you do have is less than perfect, some new knowledge of the issues is better than none at all. Finding out where the gaps are in the information is the first step in building a plan to collect better data in the future. In the worst case, where there is almost no useful data, you have to fall back on the experience of your managers and staff by raising the issue of wellbeing at work and collecting information from discussions and focus groups.

Qualitative and Quantitative Data

Understanding the health dynamics of your organisation there-fore requires two different types of data collection. On the one hand it is necessary to *quantify* the extent of the problems and their manifestations. Where are the issues? How much of a problem are they? How much do they cost us? Who is affected? Is it getting better or worse? It is also necessary to gather *qualitative* information to help understand why the issues have become issues. This is 'softer' data, information collected from discussions with managers, focus groups on health and inter-views with employees. What do we believe is causing our problems? What is our prevailing culture regarding sickness and absence? Are our policies understood? This qualitative informa-tion puts the flesh on the bare bones of the quantitative data and helps to focus attention on the key issues.

Collecting the Right Data

Information on employee wellbeing is therefore all around you and so the first step is to review the extent and accessibility of current data. Where does it sit within the organisation? Who collects it and how is it collected? This needs to be accompanied by an honest appraisal of the weaknesses and strengths in the data. This short piece of work will usually highlight what is currently not measured at all ('... the trouble is we have no data at all on...'), as well as giving some indication as to what is being collected but could be recorded better.

The best example of this is sickness absence data. When asked what sickness data they have, companies often proudly produce data files which contain information on all the absences taken by their employees in the last twelve months: day of the week taken, duration of absence, length of service, shift, and department. Frequently, however, what is missing is the reason for the absence. Sometimes a reason code is there but, on investigation, the list of codes they are selected from is too small to do any meaningful analysis of the data that has accumulated.

There is good reason for this. Most absence data collection systems were geared towards administering reclaimable statutory sick pay, where incidence and duration of absence were more important than the reason. Companies have often done a very good job measuring their absence rates, but are still unable to do anything with the data because it lacks the 'health' information needed to make it health data. In many organisations sickness absence data is believed to give an indication of sickness. It doesn't. Sickness absence data gives information about *absence*. This is an important distinction – the emphasis is usually on the time spent away from work, not the real reason why the employee wasn't present. Although we have used the term sickness absence in this book, it is a misnomer. We should be using the term absence management or, more positively, attendance management.

This is the relevance of both qualitative and quantitative information. Understanding the health dynamics of your organisation means there is a need to supplement data collection on the pure quantification of incidence with the collection of more qualitative information that will provide a clearer picture of what is really going on.

Measuring the Vital Signs

Busy managers need 'dashboard' indicators of the wellbeing of their employees; a snapshot of the people side of the business. Adopting a strategic approach to health and collecting data enable a comprehensive set of measures to be presented to the organisation. We know that levels of employee wellbeing manifest themselves in many ways and that if attendance is managed by penalising and threatening employees, then the problems surface in other ways. Management reports that simply record levels of absence or levels of labour turnover do not give a comprehensive picture. It's like looking at the results of a cricket match and trying to decide if a particular team is doing well or badly on the basis of the number of men that are out. It may be interesting to know that there are six men out, but it doesn't tell us anything unless we know how many runs they've scored and how that compares with the number of runs scored by the other team and how many men they have lost.

Each organisation will be able to build up its own 'picture of health' or the 'vital signs measure'. Figure 5.1 gives an example of

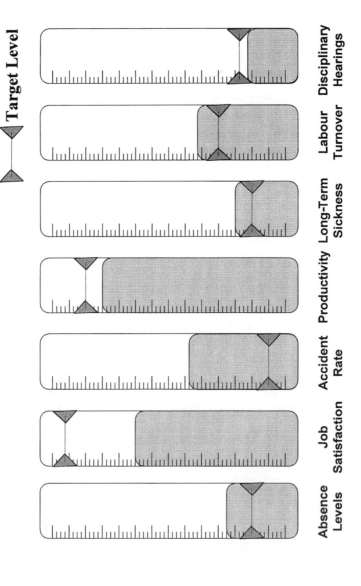

Figure 5.1 Vital signs of employee wellbeing

several dimensions of employee wellbeing that can be made available to line managers either on a company-wide or departmental level. Some of the more common measures to be included are the obvious employee wellness indicators of absence, labour turnover and accident statistics. Ill health or medical retirements should also be included, as should a measure of industrial relations activity, grievance or disciplinary procedures. Measures of productivity are increasingly difficult to find unless the organisation can use information such as sales performance, manufacturing productivity or customer satisfaction levels. Quality measures may also be a useful indicator of the 'health' of the business.

Pulling together the various measures of wellbeing can help the understanding of how they interrelate and how they change in relation to one another over time. For example, does one measure increase as another decreases? Does quality go down as staff turnover increases? One organisation used this sort of information to monitor the relationship between controlling absence levels and the impact on accident rates and industrial relations problems. The business decided to take a tough approach to absence. This resulted in a drop in the absence rate in one particular area, but a corresponding increase in accidents and industrial relations problems.

These vital signs indicators are useful, but can be difficult to set up and manage. In addition to the problems in collecting the data and ensuring accuracy, care needs to be taken in interpreting the data because of time lags in the system. In the previous example, the clampdown on absence also started to manifest itself as an increase in labour turnover, but not until several months later. As we've already seen, it can take time for people to change jobs. As more data is collected and the techniques become more sophisticated, it is possible to demonstrate the effect of the lags on the system and make connections between cause and effect that may not be immediately obvious. The time that really matters if we are correlating data on staff turnover is the point at which people decide to enter the labour market, not the date when they leave.

Benchmarking Absence Data

One good way of measuring the extent to which your absence levels are high or low is to compare your results with benchmark data from other organisations. This information is readily available; for example, the Industrial Society conducts regular surveys of sickness absence that enables an organisation to compare their own absence levels with Industrial Society data. The comparative data can be broken down according to the type of work that the employees perform and, if appropriate, factors such as gender differences, age differences and geographic differences can be controlled.

Sickness Absence Calculations

The CBI and the Labour Force surveys are also good sources of comparative data and provide benchmark data according to job type, by sector and by occupational group. The critical factor in accurate benchmarking is to ensure that the calculations are made on the same basis as the benchmark data and that data is recorded as accurately as possible. The old adage of 'Garbage In Garbage Out' applies to the analysis of sickness absence data as it does for any other information. The most commonly accepted formula for calculating sickness absence is as follows:

Calculate the number of days lost divided by the number of available working days per year, calculated as the number of full-time equivalent employees multiplied by the number of available working days per annum, usually 228. In some organisations such as the National Health Service, the formula is the hours lost divided by the hours available and this is analysed by department, job type, and so on.

When the company understands the effect of ill health on its organisation, when it starts to measure absence levels or other health risk data, it gains information that needs to be acted upon. Measurement prompts management into action. Hard evidence of levels of employee wellbeing can become another indicator of business success. Unfortunately, many employers simply ignore the problem. Others approach the issues on a superficial level and deal with the symptoms not the causes. They look at the incidence of sickness absence as evidence of individual vulner-ability, not of underlying problems in the workplace. Using the tools to diagnose, measure and raise awareness of the problems, it is possible for an organisation to identify patterns and, in time, the underlying causes and therefore adopt a health strategy that deals with the root causes of illness and poor wellbeing.

Using Absence Data to Identify 'At Risk' Areas and 'At Risk' Individuals

Frequency and Duration of Absence

As well as looking at the absence levels measured in terms of time off work, much more information can be gained about the nature of the absence by analysing the data in terms of frequency and duration. Frequency of absence is the number of absences, irrespective of the length of absence per person, per year. The duration is the number of days lost per person, per year irrespective of the number of incidences of absence. Analysis of company absence data shows that there tends to be a high level of variability in absence statistics. Simply looking at the averages and ignoring the distribution of absence can mask clusters of individuals who report much worse absence levels than their colleagues. Carrying out a cluster analysis of absence as shown in Figure 5.2, also enables the outliers, i.e. those people who have an unusually long period of absence, to be identified and, if appropriate, removed from the statistics. In the example shown, the person marked at point A has clearly had one long period of illness. In this particular individual's case the absence was the result of a heart attack, followed by a long period of convalescence. This one individual's absence level distorts the average picture for the whole department and, if not identified as an outlier, would have caused questions to be raised about the average absence levels and in turn the morale issues, and subsequently the management of that department. As expected, much of the absence is short term, with the highest concentration being people with one period of absence lasting less than 3 days. The chart also highlights a problem with one individual, person

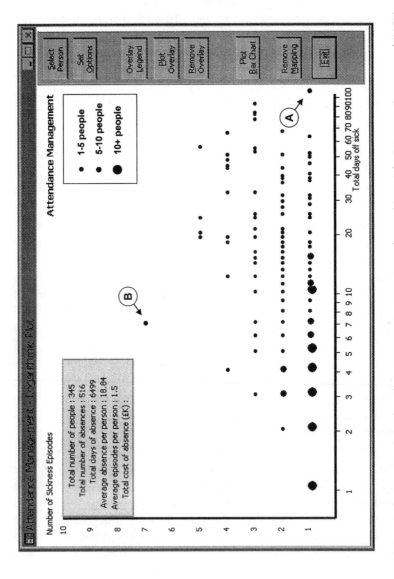

Figure 5.2 *Cluster analysis – view from the Absence Mapper computer software (Copyright Resource Systems and IHC Strategy, 1999)*

B, who has had a high number of short-term absences, possibly indicating wellbeing issues.

The computer systems that generate these 'pictures of absence' can provide the facility to 'drill down' into the data by filtering to show one department or grade or by picking up on an individual absence episode and revealing all the associated health data.

Internal Comparisons of Absence Data

Larger organisations have a wealth of information available to them that can aid their understanding of sickness absence. Absence data can be analysed by location, grade, job type, department, age, sex and so on, or by any meaningful combination of these categories. As with the external bench-marking, the internal analysis of absence data is designed to help the organisation understand the nature and extent of absence. Each group of employees is compared in terms of their reasons for absence, frequency of absence and duration of absence. The results for each group are compared with the company average and the exceptions highlighted. Groups with the highest levels of absence can then be investigated to identify potential problems in the workplace or even aspects of the work environment that are causing ill health in the employees. Particular clusters of similar reasons can also shed light on which specific disease management or self-help programmes would be of benefit. The better than average groups should also be investigated to see if there are any elements of best practice that can be identified and subsequently applied to the rest of the organisation. The point to note here is that the data is used to increase understanding of the issues by all parties and build towards a strategy for improving the situation. All too often the approach taken is not so positive. League tables are developed and circulated to 'shame' line managers to force their employees to attend more often. This is not the outcome we would wish to create.

Measuring the Absence Gap

One large organisation's occupational health team has carried out an enormous amount of work in analysing their absence data. They are responsible for the health and wellbeing of a very large number of employees working in many different businesses. The occupational health team developed their in-house version of 'dashboard measures of health'. These measures enable the business to gain a detailed understanding of employee health and wellbeing. The use of sophisticated computer models enabled the occupational health team to identify areas at risk and highlight the key characteristics of the 'at risk' group.

When this organisation compared their average sickness absence levels with those of the average in the Industrial Society survey, they were able to measure and estimate a cost for the gap between their levels of absence and the benchmark levels. The company found that the gap was costing the company several millions pounds per year. In making the financial case for improved management of employee health, the occupational health team were able to translate their actions into a simple and understandable target. If they improve sickness absence to the Industrial Society benchmark level, they will add millions of pounds to the bottom line of the business per year.

This analysis can be worked in many different ways. The objective is to show the financial benefit of improving employee wellbeing by a reduction in the relatively simple-to-measure cost of absence. Organisations at the average should compare themselves with 'best in class' and demonstrate the cost benefit to the organisation in achieving best in class status on sickness absence. For those organisations that are leading the field, the ones that are already outperforming other businesses, they can justify and measure their contribution to business profitability by comparing themselves with the average for their industry sector. For example, a company with a payroll cost of £10 million a year and sickness absence levels of 10% should acknowledge the fact that if they reduce absence levels to 6% this will add at least £400 000 pounds per year to the company's profitability.

Measure–Analyse–Intervene Model

There is little point in measurement for measurement's sake. The purpose of all this measurement is to be able to effectively map the real issues with a view to building the strategies to address them.

In his excellent book *The Mind of the Strategist*, Kenichi Ohmae stresses the importance of analysis as the key to building successful strategy:

> Analysis is the critical starting point of strategic thinking. Faced with problems that appear to constitute a harmonious whole...the strategic thinker dissects them into their constituent parts. Then, having discovered the significance of these constituents, he reassembles them in a way calculated to maximise his advantage.

This is key — if employee health is not broken down into manageable parts, it is difficult to see how it could be managed. Segmentation of the issues, coupled with the right type of investigation into some of the specific areas that combine to form the overall picture of health, can greatly simplify the route to the solutions. It is no good trying to assess where you want to be with corporate health before you have fully understood where you are now.

Once you have dissected some of the issues and gained a clearer picture of which ones are the most troublesome in terms of absence, cost or any other index, it will become very much clearer which intervention strategies need to be developed (Figure 5.3).

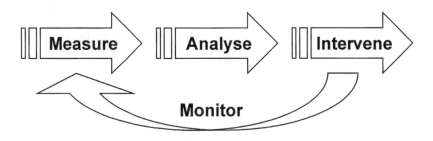

Figure 5.3   *Measure–Analyse–Intervene model*

Measurement Tools – Understanding the Why as well as the What

The Relationship Between Cause and Effect

As we have said, there are two aspects of measurement – what's happening and what's causing it to happen. It is important to quantify the effect of poor wellbeing in order to know how much of a problem it is. How prevalent is it and what does it cost us when it occurs? But knowing what poor wellbeing costs isn't enough. In order to take appropriate action we need to know what factors contribute toward the problem and, if possible, identify causal relationships between these issues and poor wellbeing outcomes.

The need for increased understanding of cause and effect is illustrated by the difficulty organisations have when they try to unlock the issue of occupational stress. Without approaching the issue in the right way, understanding the extent to which stress is a problem is extremely difficult. Stress exists in the minds of those who experience it, and each stress response is different to the next. The catalyst for stress in an individual will differ between individuals and between work groups. We cannot generalise from our own experience and we cannot assume that the issues that create stress in us will produce the same response in others. One person's role ambiguity is another's job autonomy. You may feel that you are able to 'sense' the stress in your organisation, but the chances are you are only seeing what meets your mental picture of what stress looks like. Many of the known stressors are not factors that would necessarily create a stress response in you, so you do not see them. Even if you could anticipate what is driving the stress in your company, could you prove it? Occupational stress is itself driven by a myriad of interrelated factors which then go on to affect organisational effectiveness in as many interrelated ways again. Stress is a good example to use to demonstrate the logic of the approach for, with its multivariate sources and complex interrelationships, it is, in a way, a microcosm of the overall issue of employee wellbeing. If tackled without a proper understanding of the issues and the relationship between the issues, it is unlikely that you will be able to make much headway.

Worse still, you can spend quite a significant amount of money going in the wrong direction.

Understanding complex health and wellbeing issues such as stress raises the perennial problem of causality. Does stress at work, for example, cause poor working relationships or do poor relationships cause stress? Wherever you look there are complex interrelationships between events and outcomes. We know that poor communications can be a source of stress for many people and we also know that when people are suffering from stress they tend to become uncommunicative and distant. Which comes first?

We conducted a study in a financial service organisation that neatly illustrated this point. The business was concerned about very high levels of absence in one of their sales administration areas. The analysis showed that one of the most significant factors driving absence was work overload. The reason that there was too much work was that there were too few people to do it. People were too busy covering for their colleagues to do their own work and the nature of the job meant that the paperwork had to be processed immediately. It couldn't be delayed until the absentee returned. The only way people could cope was by taking time off and, of course, this added to the problem. The employees were locked in a vicious circle where absence caused workload pressure that caused absence that caused workload pressure and so on.

The solution in this case was to break the loop, to find a way of temporarily balancing workload with capacity until absence levels could be reduced. A temporary fix broke the cycle, but other steps had to be taken to ensure that the situation didn't deteriorate again. This required a different level of analysis. It meant monitoring the absence levels over time and identifying the links to external events. For example, the managers had found that changes in legislation produced a significant increase in workload while the internal systems were adjusted to comply with the new regulations. However, they believed that this was a temporary effect. If the data analysis shows that absence levels increase as workload increases, the organisation has now identified an event that has long-term consequences for the business. The managers can now demonstrate that what may appear to be a temporary increase in workload actually has a long-term effect. Knowing this, the business can then allocate extra resources to pre-empt the problem. By continuing to collect data, the business can measure the extent to which a short-term increase in resources prevents a long-term increase in absence levels.

The only way, therefore, to really understand wellbeing issues is by the analysis of longitudinal data, data collected over months or years that can show causal relationships. Data that can be linked to external events as well as to other 'health' data and analysed to show how a change in one part of the business may have profound effects elsewhere. Chaos theory really does have something to teach us about the management of health. Correlation is not the same as causation − only by collecting data over time can you really make sense of the factors that influence wellbeing at work. It also follows that the data you collect needs to be consistent.

Using the Right Tools

The need to understand the cause-and-effect relationship makes it necessary to invest more than just time in finding out more about the hidden issues and discover what is really going on below the water-line. As we have said, detailed analysis of what is going on now, combined with an awareness of what is below the surface, is the key to moving towards the most appropriate and most cost-efficient solutions. By definition, what is not immediately visible is more difficult to measure and it may be necessary to elicit some help in collecting the right information and collecting it consistently.

Health Risk Appraisal

One of the most easily available methods of collecting information on employee wellbeing is a health risk appraisal (HRA) questionnaire. Either paper questionnaire or interactive PC based, this approach seeks to collect information at the individual employee level about current health issues and health risks. Most diseases develop slowly in the presence of various risk factors, which are either genetic or behavioural. Health risk appraisal tools collect this information by asking each participating employee a series of questions about their lifestyle and their medical history. This information is then processed confidentially by the supplier and usually results in the production of a personal report for the employee. This will detail their own unique profile of health risks, as well as providing guidance on where they could best direct their efforts to improve their health status. Where there are sufficient numbers of participating employees, the data can then be aggregated to produce a company health profile. This will map the distribution of health issues and health-related behavioural patterns across the business and so provide both a valuable image of the hidden health issues and which interventions will be most effective.

Where the survey has been of sufficient size and demographic data allows, reports can be produced to show trends and patterns between different departments, workplace locations, job function and so on. For those companies interested in benchmarking, some providers can also present the company's own data alongside national averages.

One of the benefits of using tools like these is that they make it possible to snatch more than a glimpse of the issues that, to use our analogy again, are hidden beneath the waves. They reveal the prevalence of lifestyle behaviours that could create the ill health that will drive the sickness absences of the future. This is important because health interventions cost less and are more effective the earlier you apply them. Most employers do not get the chance to intervene or assist their employees in the early stages because they do not know that the issue is there. Measurement tools that allow you to see the health risks hidden beneath the water-line can clearly help us get to the issues when they are less costly to treat and before they have cost the organisation and the employee.

These measurement tools also give the employer a chance to know more about the current health status of employees. Remember that not all ill health manifests itself as an absence. Employers who have completed HRA programmes have said that they were surprised at the numbers of employees who suffered from chronic conditions like migraine and diabetes. Some of these show up as sickness absences, but many do not. Knowing that these medical conditions exist gives valuable insight into which health interventions are likely to be valued as well as where we can impact on absence by helping employees to manage their condition better.

Stress Audits

A stress audit is a specific form of health risk appraisal. It is a structured approach to investigating and analysing the component parts of the stress process. A stress audit uses a well-validated questionnaire to collect information from a large number of employees. The questionnaire measures factors such as the sources of pressure. For example, workload, relationships at work, life/work balance, personal responsibility, recognition and the extent people feel valued, and everyday hassles and irritants. The questionnaire should also measure the extent to which the various pressures reported by an individual are moderated or amplified by personality or behavioural differences. This involves measuring drive or impatience, the extent someone feels they have control over events and the level of discretion they have in their jobs. It is also necessary to measure the way that people cope with pressure. Do they focus on the problem itself and use time or risk management skills to deal with the underlying issues? Do they rely on talking to other people and sharing their problems with friends or relatives? Alternatively, they may be able to separate themselves from the emotion of the problem and avoid stress by being calm and detached. Finally, a stress audit measures the outcomes of the stress process, the effects of pressure on the employee. A comprehensive audit will measure not just the mental or physical health outcomes but also the 'morale' issues such as job and organisational satisfaction and organisational commitment and security.

Figure 5.4 shows the components of a stress audit conducted using a well-known questionnaire, the Pressure Management Indicator.

Employee Opinion Surveys

The most widely used organisational measurement tools areemployee opinion or attitude surveys. These surveys use questionnaires to measure various aspects of organisational

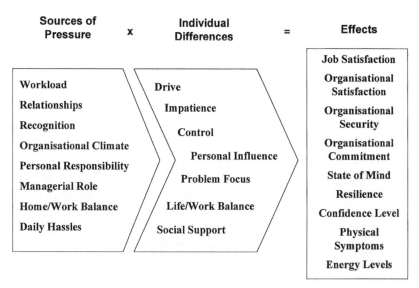

| Sources of Pressure | x | Individual Differences | = | Effects |

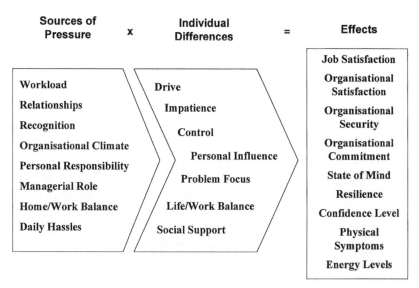

Figure 5.4 *The Pressure Management Indicator measurement domains*

climate, employee satisfaction, morale, working environment, culture and so on. Some organisations develop and analyse their own questionnaires, others subscribe to a standardised survey instrument designed and analysed by an organisational survey provider. The obvious benefit of using an external provider is the ability to benchmark your organisation's data with that of other businesses, usually in the same industry sector. However, an over-reliance on benchmarking can seriously limit the value of the data. It may be useful to know that your company is in the lower quartile with regard to employee satisfaction but, unless the survey clearly identifies the issues that determine satisfaction in your organisation, it will not help you to focus on the most beneficial interventions.

Attitude surveys should be designed to provide a comprehensive measurement of the way employees feel about the organisation and should contain enough demographic detail to enable the data to be analysed according to location, job type, grade, gender and so on. Because attitude surveys are usually completed anonymously, it may not be possible to link the results to other organisational variables such as labour turnover, sickness absence or performance unless detailed demographic information is also collected. For example, the average level of satisfaction with the way people are managed may hide severe problems in one division, department or location. A more detailed analysis of the results may show a problem in one specific department that can be linked to other factors such as higher levels of staff turnover or poor quality in that department. Further analysis of the departmental data may help focus on some of the specific issues leading to dissatisfaction with, for example, management style. Although it is important to safeguard the anonymity of individual employees, the survey data is most useful when it can be analysed by the smallest collection of employees, usually work teams. To follow the reef analogy, the survey results may show that there are problems in the organisation, that we are entering dangerous waters. The more detailed the analysis, the clearer the picture and the more precise we can be about the nature and extent of the hazards.

USING DATA

Data Integration

A single measurement of one aspect of employee wellbeing is unlikely to be either reliable or accurate. All measurement contains error and, in order for the data to be useful, we have to reduce the level of error and quantify the extent of the error. If we don't go through this process we have no idea if the effect we are reporting is a true reflection of employee wellbeing or a function of badly-worded questions. We have seen organisations invest millions of pounds in running surveys without evaluating the reliability and validity of their questionnaires. In the worst cases, badly-worded questionnaires lead to false conclusions about the nature of the problem and a complete waste of resources trying to fix problems that don't exist. As well as using statistical techniques such as item analysis or confirmatory factor analysis to evaluate the survey questionnaires, organisations should collect data from a variety of sources and link them together to give a comprehensive picture. The power of data integration is revealed when measurements from several different instruments are combined with known outcomes such as staff turnover or attendance levels so that errors can be identified and causal relationships discovered. Combining data from many different sources and analysing it in such a way as to reveal the underlying structure and causal relationships turns raw data into useful information.

In our work with organisations, we have become increasingly aware that simple averages are usually meaningless. The larger the group that is being analysed, the more the data will revert to the mean and the more it will hide specific issues within subgroups. For example, one financial services organisation carried out a stress audit in several divisions. The average level of satisfaction with the organisation in their customer services division was about the same as for other organisations. However, further analysis showed massive differences between departments within this division. The average masked deep dissatisfaction in one particular area. Further analysis of this 'problem' department again revealed significant differences according to job type, with one particular group of employees, the processing staff, being particularly unhappy. The need to take action to improve satisfaction for this particular group of workers was confirmed by their higher than average absence levels and, more revealingly, the high number of requests to transfer to other departments within the organisation. Detailed statistical analysis of data from several sources was used to identify the critical issues driving dissatisfaction, and action was taken to deal directly with these key issues. A superficial analysis of the results would have led the organisation to believe that they were 'about average' for their industry sector and didn't need to do anything.

Integrated Health Risk Appraisal

The more precisely data can be linked, the more useful the information and the greater the probability of identifying causal relationships. Although integrating data at a departmental level is useful, the analysis will always be confounded by missing data and changing populations. For example, not everyone who completes an HRA questionnaire will complete a stress audit or an organisational climate questionnaire. If this is the case we will not know if the differences in the results are due to different methods of measurement or different people completing the questionnaires? When trying to link survey data to absence levels or staff turnover, the results will not be particularly useful if the people who are absent or are thinking of leaving the organisation are the ones who don't complete the questionnaire. The ideal is to be able to correlate data at the individual employee level. This enables changes to be monitored using different measures at different times, and demographic differences that may bias the results such as grade levels or gender can be controlled.

The most effective way of integrating data is to combine a series of questionnaires into one survey instrument. Some of the most effective work in this area has been carried out by Dr Robert Willcox and his occupational health team at Cable & Wireless in the UK. They offer a comprehensive integrated questionnaire to all of their staff annually. The Cable & Wireless Health Check Questionnaire measures the following aspects of health:

- Demographic details.
- Clinical details (height, weight; BP and cholesterol if known).
- Smoking:
  - if a smoker, questions on giving up, also questions to determine whether an attempt to quit is likely;
  - if an ex-smoker, questions on how gave up.
- Alcohol:
  - if a drinker, questions on drinking pattern, units consumed and personal feelings about alcohol.
- Eyesight:
  - if a wearer of glasses/contact lens, what type and how long worn.
- Current exercise level (perceived).
- Sleep (quality and length).
- Exercise prescription (comprising):
  - current state of health (surgery details, heart event details, joint problem details, other specific current health questions);
  - exercise habits (recent levels of exercise over the last seven days);
  - aims and objectives (of exercising).

- Headaches:
  - basic causes of stress (commuting, shift working, etc.);
  - headache associations;
  - if suffering from headaches:
    - severity;
    - symptoms;
    - warning signs;
    - treatment and preventative drugs;
    - time off work.
- Managing pressure:
  - job and organisational satisfaction;
  - organisational security and commitment;
  - mental and physical wellbeing;
  - sources of pressure;
  - drive and impatience;
  - control and influence;
  - coping and support.
- Working time/life events:
  - working practices;
  - recent major life events;
  - general health and recent illness.

To encourage participation, each employee receives a computer-generated personal profile with the results of the questionnaire. Because the data is coded by employee number, it is possible to link the questionnaire results with information from the human resource or health database. Clearly, the need to protect employee confidentiality is of paramount importance and the questionnaire data is held exclusively by occupational health and not shared with human resource or line management. Other organisations overcome the confidentiality issues by having their data scored and analysed by an external provider who has contracted not to supply details of any individual to the organisation.

Analysing the Data

Once the data has been collated and linked, it can be analysed. In our experience, very few organisations make full use of the data they have. Analysis, even of sophisticated attitude survey data, is often superficial and limited to reporting the proportion of employees that agree or disagree with a particular statement. In many cases, the surveys report on broader concepts such as an overall measure of job satisfaction, but the items contributing to this scale have simply been put together because they seem to fit, not because the data has been factor analysed to show underlying structure. The use of more sophisticated statistical techniques such as regression analysis or structural equation modelling can clarify the relations between the variables and highlight causal relationships when applied to data collected over time. Figure 5.5 illustrates the use of structural equation modelling in the analysis of factors responsible for the 'uplifts' and the 'hassles' influencing employee satisfaction.

The easiest way to understand this model is to think of the items in the boxes as being towns and the lines as roads connecting the towns. The arrows show that the traffic can flow in only one direction. The circles on the diagram are like roundabouts, they allow you to continue on the existing road or turn on to another road. For example, to understand the impact that supportive leadership has on individual morale, the diagram shows that it has an influence on appraisal and recognition and that in turn influences professional growth. The numbers with circles around them show what proportion of the variation in outcome the model cannot explain. For example, (22) pointing to workplace morale shows that 78% of the variation in workplace morale can be explained by the model and 22% is unexplained.

The route for professional growth leads to individual morale. Following the left-hand path from supportive leadership, we can see it also has an impact on role clarity and that role clarity in turn is linked to individual morale. There is no direct link between supportive leadership and individual morale and the model suggests that the effect of supportive leadership is moderated by appraisal and recognition systems, the opportunities for professional growth and, as a separate issue, role clarity. Following the pathway from individual morale, round the outside of the diagram, we can see that it is linked to excessive work demands. A combination of low individual morale and excessive work demands leads to individual and workplace distress.

The model reveals that there is no relationship between

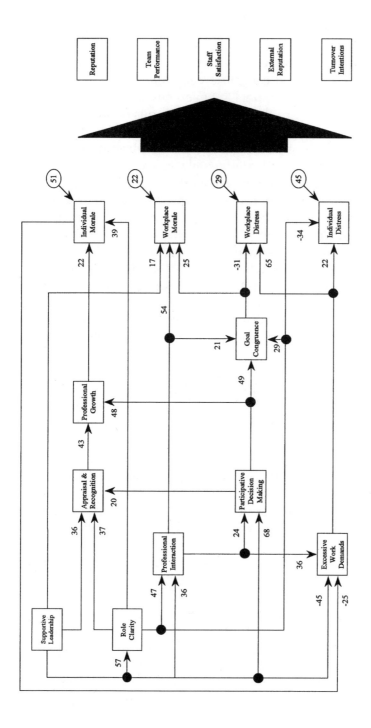

Figure 5.5 *Structural equation modelling – how does supportive leadership function? (Source: P.M. Hart, Social Research Consultants, Melbourne)*

excessive work demands and workplace or individual morale. This may seem counter-intuitive until we think about the issues in more depth. Work demands influence both individual and workplace distress and can cause people to feel tired, worn out, suffer from stress and so on. However, despite all these pressures and despite the cost to the individual in terms of their mental and physical wellbeing, morale can still be high. We see this in a number of high-pressured organisations where workload takes its toll on individual health but people enjoy their jobs and the organisation and are highly committed to what they do. The model demonstrates that one of the factors influencing the perception that work demands are excessive is actually low individual morale; the explanation is that if morale is low, we are more likely to interpret workplace pressures and demands as excessive than if morale is high, and it's that change in perception that leads to the stress outcome. Put simply, in this particular organisation there is evidence to show that low morale combined with a lack of supportive leadership would increase the perception that work demands are excessive and that would, in turn, lead to stress. A simple interpretation, based perhaps on anecdote or observation, would be that the organisation had to reduce the workload, either by taking on less work or by recruiting more people. The model suggests that simply reducing the amount of work would not, on its own, significantly improve the situation and could be an expensive mistake.

At first sight the model may appear confusing and we may puzzle over some of the interrelationships between the factors. This kind of modelling does, however, clarify many of the assumptions we make about the causal relationships in business. Although we've not shown the relationship between morale, distress and independently measured outcomes of performance indicators such as team performance, satisfaction, the internal reputation of a department, the external reputation, profit performance, customer service levels and so on, all of these relationships can be established empirically. The power of the model is that it not only makes the relationships between variables explicit, but it quantifies those relationships. For example, we can see from Figure 5.5 that there is a strong positive relationship between supportive leadership and partici-pative decision making (68) and between supportive leadership and role clarity (57). However, the relationship between supportive leadership and workplace morale is much lower (17).

The table in Figure 5.6 shows the same information in a more accessible form. It is derived from the above model and simply shows each of the factors we wish to influence: individual and workplace morale, and individual and workplace distress, and rank orders the factors that contribute to those particular outcomes and their relative strengths. The diagram shows that supportive leadership is the main determinant of workplace morale and also has an impact on individual and workplace distress, individual distress and individual morale. An organisation with limited resources would therefore expect to see improvements in all of these areas, particularly workplace morale, by introducing a programme to develop and enhance supportive leadership. However, Figure 5.5 reminds us that interventions to improve supportive leadership will give maximum benefit when combined with improvements in appraisal and recognition systems and creating opportunities for professional growth.

Carrying out this kind of detailed analysis of the workplace and the relationship between factors the organisation can control and performance-related outcomes looks complicated. However, once the systems are in place, the analysis can be carried out for different work groups and repeated over time to measure the effect of intervention programmes. These techniques can be used to get management teams to think about the relationships between variables and to redirect resources into areas that will give maximum payback. Understanding the real relationships will avoid wasting money on interventions that, even if they were done perfectly, would have little or no impact on the outcomes the organisation wishes to influence.

This particular model is interesting because it shows that the factors responsible for promoting individual and workplace morale are different from the factors that lead to individual and workplace distress. It quantifies the relationship between the fact that people can, at the same time, enjoy their work and suffer from stress. If the organisation wants to improve morale it has to remove or reduce the irritants. To encourage people to enjoy their jobs it also has to continue to provide or enhance the uplifts. Without more sophisticated analysis of the data it wouldn't be obvious that the things that make people happy in

Individual Morale		Individual Distress		Workplace Morale		Workplace Distress	
Role Clarity	44	Emotionality	61	Supportive Leadership	69	Excessive Work Demands	65
Supportive Leadership	38	Role Clarity	-33	Professional Interaction	63	Supportive Leadership	-43
Emotionality	-28	Supportive Leadership	-27	Role Clarity	37	Emotionality	40
Sociability	27	Excessive Work Demands	22	Goal Congruence	25	Goal Congruence	-31
Professional Growth	22			Emotionality	-24	Participative Decision Making	-17
Participative Decision Making	13			Participative Decision Making	12	Individual Morale	-16
Appraisal and Recognition	10			Sociability	11	Professional Interaction	13
						Role Clarity	-10

Figure 5.6   *Major determinants of individual and workplace distress and morale (Source: P.M. Hart, Social Research Consultants, Melbourne)*

their work are not the opposites of the things that make them unhappy. Both factors are important, but they are important in different ways.

SUMMARY

Measurement is the key to managing wellbeing at work. Without measurement there is no understanding of the real issues, no way of calculating the cost and no opportunity to show improvement. We have seen that measuring health is difficult, imprecise and may not be seen as a priority for the business. In the absence of a model of best practice that works for all organisations all of the time, you have to start with what you've got and progress from there. Measuring health issues will show you what's happening to your people in your organisation. It enables you to identify the key drivers for health that are specific to your situation at that point in time and design appropriate interventions based on understanding not hearsay. By linking your wellbeing data to external events and business metrics over time, you will be able to assess the impact of change and improve the relevance of your interventions. Subsequent measurements will act as a performance indicator showing how much you have accomplished and how well the interventions have worked.

Measurement tools are the organisation's depth counter. They may not be 100% accurate or precise but they provide a glimpse of what lies below the surface. Measuring may not be easy but it's the place to start any health intervention. Begin with the end in mind and collect, analyse and interpret data to reveal the hidden dangers and use this information to steer a safe course.

6
Improving Individual Health

The first half of this book has examined the issues that have either a direct or an indirect influence on wellbeing at work. We have explored the reasons for which we believe wellbeing is one of the most critical issues facing organisations today and how it can be analysed in terms of the visible and hidden costs to the business. The second half of the book discusses what can be done to improve employee wellbeing. We start with individual health and show how organisations can actively promote good health. We then look in detail at the management of attendance and offer some specific guidance on reducing sickness absence, one of the most visible manifestations of ill health. Following our reef analogy, we then look below the surface at the hidden dimensions of employee wellbeing. Chapter 9 continues to broaden the notion of wellbeing and looks at ways of improving organisational wellbeing. Finally Chapter 10 draws these varied interventions together into an integrated strategy for health.

We start this second part of the book discussing methodologies for improving individual health for a good reason. Corporate ill health is not a collective event, although the regular publication of sickness absence data at company, department and national level has encouraged organisations to see it that way. A company's sickness absence statistics are made up of thousands of individual sickness episodes – thousands of individual employees with their own personal cocktail of wellbeing issues conspiring to keep them away from work. To use the reef analogy again, the hidden issues are built up, like coral itself, from a collection of individuals. The focus on absence statistics makes it easy to lose sight of the individual in this process, but all our corporate ill health costs emanate from *individuals* with wellbeing issues. As we saw in the previous chapter, it follows that any attempt to understand the global issue must come from improving our understanding of the individual issues. Likewise, any attempt at improving health and wellbeing at work must start at the same place; with the employees themselves.

Throughout this book we emphasise the role of the organisation in managing wellbeing at work but recognise that, in the final analysis, health is the responsibility of the individual. Organisations are responsible for providing a safe and healthy workplace and should actively encourage wellbeing, but they cannot force their employees to be healthy. Each individual employee is personally responsible for the management of his or her health. Other people can help, advise, support and direct health behaviours but they can't do it for you. You need to take responsibility for changing your behaviour and improving your overall wellbeing. In order to do this, you need to understand the issues, identify what you need to change, how rapidly you need to change it, and how important it is to change. You may also need help, resources and guidance in making the change. We are all unique. We all have our individual pattern of health. We need to be aware of the dimensions of health and wellness, understand the drivers for change and be encouraged to make changes.

THE ILLNESS FULFILMENT CONTINUUM

We should begin by recognising that there is no dividing line between sickness and health. The change from wellness to illness is spread out along a continuum, as shown in Figure 6.1.

The barrier reef analogy highlighted the differences between the visible and hidden dimensions of workplace wellbeing. In the same way, the visible manifestations of ill health appearing above the surface are the outcome of a process that started far below. The employee who becomes physically or psychologically unwell has usually moved through all of the stages from exposure or possession of health risk through to the eventual

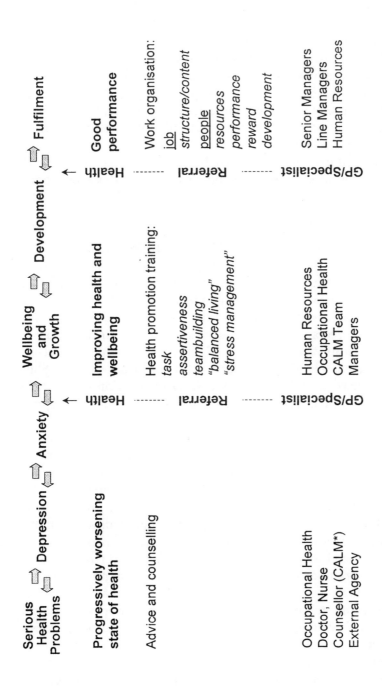

Figure 6.1 *The wellness to illness continuum – individual wellbeing/organisational success (*CALM, Counselling and Life Management) (Source: R.J. Heron and E.L. Teasdale, Zeneca Pharmaceuticals)*

sickness absence. Looking at the continuum from wellness to illness encourages people to recognise that ill health does not happen overnight, but is an accumulation of a variety of factors. Blurring the distinction between health and illness should help to shift the focus toward the maintenance of good health and early intervention. It also assists in shaping the health improvement messages. If employees are encouraged to see that health issues are continuous and can then go on to identify where they are on their individual health continuum, then the relevance and the impact of the intervention can be improved. To illustrate the point let us look at a few examples of how this can work in practice.

Fiona's Story – Physical Ill Health

Fiona is 35 years old and a customer service leader in a medium-sized company which has just completed a significant restructuring exercise. She has been working for this organisation for a number of years, developing her career from a customer service assistant to service leader. She is very committed to her job and feels passionately about the service that her team delivers. She is striving hard to build a positive working relationship with her new director, who has recently gained responsibility for her area.

She is healthy and has no history of back problems. In the terms of this model she therefore starts from the centre, only at risk from injury. At this risk stage she does not have a specific medical complaint, but she does possess a number of physical, social and behavioural characteristics that combine to increase her risk of back injury. Additionally, she has a predominantly sedentary role in the office, meaning that her employer will have considered her unlikely to be at risk from manual handling injury. She has therefore never been offered any formal training, either in the workplace or outside of work, on how to lift without putting unnecessary strain on her back. Fiona has recently returned from maternity leave and is doing a good deal of lifting during the evenings and at night, as her wakeful baby goes in and out of the car and cot.

None of these risk factors are likely to be sufficiently noticeable for her employer to be aware of them, but none the less they are there. In the second month after her return to work she sustains a back injury after lifting the baby out of the cot badly. The pain is not, however, sufficiently severe to keep her from work in the morning. She and her back are now moving to the left of the diagram, the wrong way along the continuum. As the weeks go on, the pain from the original injury worsens. The growing baby and its demands make it impossible for her to rest the injury and, because of her commitment to her job and her wish to make a good impression on her new boss, she elects not to take time off to rest and recover. The pain and discomfort during the day are growing, but she still wants to come to work and set a good example to her colleagues. She is therefore visibly at work, but her performance is now being affected. Although she is normally affable and light-hearted, her constant pain is undermining the quality of her customer interface, her people management skills and her decision making. This reduced effectiveness is, however, largely invisible to her and her employers, although her direct reports have noticed that she is more abrupt than she was previously.

This continues for some time until eventually her back problem, which remains unreported but is worsening gradually, moves her further along to the left in the continuum model and the first sick day is taken. Still anxious not to appear uncommitted, she returns after only one day off, which has little effect on her back. Over the next few weeks there are more odd days taken, with visits to the GP for painkillers and a consultation with an osteopath. Some weeks later, what she had initially thought of as a back strain that could be lived with finally renders her immobile as she lifts the baby awkwardly out of the back of her car.

She is now signed off by the GP for a period of several weeks. Worried about what is happening at work and paying for full-time child care anyway, she comes back to work in less time than the GP recommended to rest her back. She is once again at her desk, but pain continues to undermine her performance and greatly complicates her domestic responsibilities. Despite this, she continues her behaviour pattern.

Some six months later, on the advice of fellow sufferers and friends, she exercises her right to use the company medical insurance and after a series of physiotherapy treatments and osteopathy, which produce no noticeable improvement in her back pain, she persuades her GP to refer her for surgical investigation.

She has therefore moved from the centre (health) to the extreme left of the model (serious health problem) in less than one year. The early part of this process, where prompt intervention treatment and support were more likely to have controlled the problem, took place largely without the knowledge of her employer. The employer nevertheless now bears the much higher costs of her hospital treatment and has borne the cost of her sick pay and reduced performance for the whole of the period.

She and her family have paid heavily too. The additional pressure she placed on herself to 'soldier on' because of her commitment to her job, means that she has had to function on both work and home fronts while coping with pain and discomfort as well as the 'normal' stresses associated with trying to do both. This has put her relationship with her partner under considerable strain.

The point of this example is threefold. First, that the health issue was invisible but none the less real. Secondly, had it been more visible there were opportunities to intervene at each stage. Awareness of Fiona's health risks could have facilitated help and advice that might have prevented the initial injury and therefore the substantial costs to both the parties. If the injury had still occurred, but the culture of her company or attitude of her boss had discouraged presenteeism, then the injury would have been dealt with earlier and the number of days lost to treatment and recovery would have been lower. If the company had invested in a formal back-care management programme for staff, then surgery may well have been avoided through earlier physiotherapy intervention or, as above, the injury prevented through better awareness of her own combination of risks. The third point to note is that the physical injury evolved, as it moved through the continuum, into a psychosocial health problem too.

It follows therefore that better awareness of the health continuum for employees makes it possible to impact on all three aspects of health when we intervene. The provision of back-care advice would have prevented a physical injury and, by halting the progress along the continuum, also prevented the secondary social and psychological 'injuries' caused by the first. Fiona's case study describes her movement along the health continuum from the centre to the extreme left. More effective intervention would probably have prevented the deterioration in her health; positive and proactive wellbeing initiatives may also have enabled her to move to the right, towards development and fulfilment.

Megan's Story – Mental Ill Health

Our second case study describes the deterioration in an individual's wellbeing when problems at home lead to problems at work that, in turn, lead to more problems at home and more problems at work. The problem starts with a relatively minor, not uncommon concern with the wellbeing of a child and ends in major physical illness. When and how could it have been avoided?

Megan worked as clerk in the accounts department of a large manufacturing company in the Midlands. She had been with the firm for nine years and, although she got fed up occasionally, she enjoyed her job and liked the people she worked with. Things began to go wrong about a year ago when her eldest son started having problems at school. At first Megan thought it was just part of growing up – her son, like many other 15 year olds, had decided he no longer liked school and didn't want to go. He wouldn't get up in the morning and wouldn't do his homework. Mornings were frantic at the best of times as Megan rushed to get the children organised and make the breakfast before she left for work. On a couple of occasions she spent so long arguing with her son that she missed her bus and was late for work. Even when she got to work on time she was so wound up from the morning that she found it hard to concentrate, worked more slowly and made silly mistakes.

The situation got worse when Megan had a call from the school about her son's non-attendance. He had been leaving home late and felt that if he was going to be late then he may as well not go to school at all. Her son refused to talk about the situation and home became a battlefield. To add to the family problems, Megan's husband found out that there was going to be a major reorganisation at his firm and he might lose his job. He started going to work earlier and leaving later in the hope that working longer hours would improve his chances of not being made redundant.

Megan became more and more worried. She worried about her son, about her husband's job and, increasingly, about her own job. She knew that her work hadn't been up to her usual standard. She'd had to take a couple of days off to go to meetings with her son at the school and had been late a few times. She was preoccupied at work and, as well as making mistakes, she'd been offhand with other members of staff. She wasn't sleeping well, wasn't eating properly, was irritable, and felt tired and worn out all the time. Her home life was a mess, her work life was becoming a mess. Megan used to get on well with her boss and was really surprised when she was called into her office and given a warning about her work. Megan tried to explain about the family problems but she didn't really want to talk about it and, anyway, her boss made it quite clear that personal problems shouldn't affect her work.

Megan continued to worry. She found it difficult to get to sleep and kept waking in the night. She and her husband had rows all the time and her son was just impossible to live with. Her back ached, she couldn't eat and she felt dreadful. She had a few days off work but didn't feel any better, so she went to the doctor but he couldn't find anything wrong. He said she was just a bit run down and should try to get some rest. As time went on, Megan got worse. She kept getting minor illnesses, stomach problems, backache and colds. When she took time off work she just sat around at home on her own and worried even more. When she went to the office she had no interest in her work and felt that her boss was constantly criticising her. She was told that she made mistakes, her timekeeping was poor and she 'wasn't pulling her weight'. After struggling with minor illnesses for months Megan collapsed and was taken to hospital where she was diagnosed as suffering from hypertension. She was off work for six months before her employer decided that she was too ill to return and retired her on grounds of ill health.

Megan's case raises a number of questions. Was her illness avoidable? Did it have anything to do with work? Should her employer have tried to help? If so, what could her boss have done? Was her illness brought on by worry?

Megan's case may be extreme but it's by no means unusual.

Work affects home and home affects work. We can't pretend that the two aren't linked and that people shouldn't bring their personal problems to work. Many people find that problems at home lead to problems at work. In one recent study, 80% of managers found to be suffering from occupational stress could trace the start of their problems at work to events at home.

Megan's case also shows how worry or other psychological health problems can affect physical wellbeing. None of Megan's sick notes mentioned the word 'stress' or 'nervous exhaustion' or anything that would imply that her illness had a psychological component. As far as her boss was concerned the quality of Megan's work started to deteriorate, she was irritable, and her sickness absence days increased. There was no reason to think that these factors were linked. There was no reason to believe that the company should do anything to help.

Fiona and Megan both moved from wellness to illness without challenging the underlying problem or actively trying to change their response to ill health. If their employers had been more aware of the existence of the risks and the stages they were moving through as the risk became real, then they may have been able to intervene long before the issues became so costly. Similarly, if the employees themselves had been more aware of the gradual development of these health issues and of when and how they could have changed their behaviour or obtained support, they may have avoided the most destructive phase of their illness.

Readiness to Change

People vary in their willingness to change and, depending on what stage they are at, the messages and incentives for change will be different. Some of the most interesting work on changing behaviours has been carried out by two researchers working in the field of addictive behaviours. These researchers, Prochaska and DiClemente, studied smoking cessation and compared the change process undertaken by both self-changers and those attending a 'stop smoking clinic'. The major finding from their work is that behaviour change involves an individual going through several stages before change is achieved. Prochaska and

DiClemente call this the transtheoretical model. Their original work was refined by Prochaska and led to his development of a five-stage model, shown in Figure 6.2. The model identifies the five key areas as:

- Pre-contemplation.
- Contemplation.
- Preparation.
- Action.
- Maintenance.

Pre-contemplation.   Pre-contemplation is the stage where people are not considering the possibility of change. They may not be aware that they have a problem or they may deny that they have a problem. People at this stage don't see the need to change and are unlikely to take notice of any initiatives designed to promote change.

Contemplation.   The contemplation stage is where people become aware of the need to change. In the contemplation stage, people can often see the benefits of change and understand the reasons why they should, but they also see the disadvantages and are reluctant to start the change process. People at this stage are open to information and often spend time weighing up the pros and cons of change. This contemplation stage can, for many people, take a long time. Prochaska, for example, found that

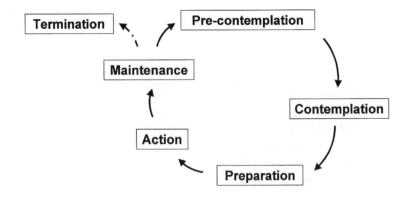

Figure 6.2   *Stages of change (Source: Prochaska and DiClemente, 1983)*

smoking self-changers might think about stopping smoking for between one and two years before actually taking action: 'I'll get round to it next week' or 'I'll wait until the summer' or other delaying excuses are often indicators that someone is in the contemplation stage.

Preparation.   In the preparation stage, people have gone beyond contemplation, decided that they should change their behaviours, and will probably start doing something differently in the next two or three months. People are preparing themselves to change but are not yet fully committed to it and are still weighing up the pros and cons. It's at the preparation stage that negative messages may tip the balance in favour of not making the change and they then don't proceed to do anything differently.

Action.   This stage is where people start to do things differently. It's when they make changes to their behaviours and start putting their thoughts into action. At this stage, people believe that because they're doing something, change will be inevitable and will be lasting. People may, for example, be absolutely certain that they've given up smoking, drinking excessively, overeating or not taking enough exercise. The problem is that for a large number of people, the action phase is temporary. Behaviour change isn't successful unless it's lasting and, having taken action, people need to realise that they cannot be complacent and need to continue to work at successful change.

Maintenance.   This is where the maintenance of change comes into play. Action has been taken and behaviours are different, but people need to recognise the importance of maintaining their changed state. It's at this point that people, particularly those who have been through the change process before, start to worry about relapsing. They question how long they will be able to continue and small setbacks such as smoking one cigarette or missing one exercise period can make them believe that they've failed. Sometimes people stay at the maintenance stage for ever. For example, some alcoholics may feel that they always have to fight against slipping back into their old behaviours and never reach the point where they regard themselves as being free of temptation.

The other two aspects of the model are the outcomes of the change process. The negative outcome is relapse. This is where the individual slips out of the stage of change at some point and relapses back into the old behaviours. For many people going into the change process, relapsing and starting the change process again is a continuing cycle. The old joke about the smoker who claims that stopping smoking is easy because 'I've given up 30 times already' illustrates the change–relapse–change–relapse–change cycle.

The other outcome, the positive outcome, is termination. At the termination stage, the cycle of change is broken. The new behaviours are more powerful than the old behaviours and the change process is no longer relevant.

Why Stages of Change Are Important

There is clear and convincing evidence to show that changing behaviours improves health. There seems little doubt that stopping smoking, avoiding excessive drinking and taking up regular physical activity improves health and wellbeing. For example, it's been found that physically active individuals have half the risk of coronary heart disease compared with non-active people. In spite of all the evidence supporting regular exercise and healthier eating, the population in most Western countries is becoming less active and more obese. A recent report stated that over 60% of Americans are now classified as obese. In order to combat lack of activity and deterioration in health, an enormous amount of effort has been put into promoting the benefits of regular exercise. It's also been found that much of this activity is wasted because approximately 50% of adults taking up exercise programmes will drop out within three to six months.

Employers can be extremely influential in helping individuals to take up exercise and change their health behaviours. They are better able to target those groups of people least likely to respond to public health campaigns, such as older people and people with low incomes. The problem with most exercise programmes at work is that they tend to attract those people who are already most highly motivated or physically active. Many fitness centre managers accept that the success of their facilities is often dependent on the number of people who have shifted where they take their exercise. Instead of going to the local gym or fitness centre they now use the work facilities. Attracting those people who have never exercised is extremely difficult. Organisations then find that they have spent hundreds of thousands of pounds on installing a state-of-the-art fitness centre, recruiting highly experienced and highly motivated staff and the net outcome is a negligible improvement in the activity levels of the majority of the workforce. Indeed it is often said that one of the main reasons why people who are inactive don't use the fitness centre is that all the fit, healthy, athletic individuals that go there put them off. It's very difficult for an overweight, older, unfit person wearing a baggy jogging suit to feel good when they're on an exercise machine next to a young, attractive, fit person dressed in figure-hugging Lycra! Employers then need to understand that providing the facilities is not the same as effecting the change. It is part of the story but not all of it.

Mary's Story – The Stages of Change

The following case study is an example of someone working through the stages of change as they move towards a healthier lifestyle that includes regular exercise.

Mary hadn't taken regular exercise since her teens. At the age of 37 she was slightly overweight but she ate well, watched her diet, and went on the occasional bike ride with her children. A number of her friends were members of local gyms or fitness centres and she had started an aerobics class but found it difficult to fit in with her busy home and work life and hadn't really enjoyed it anyway. Mary's company had a fitness centre and although she'd seen the posters and the features in the company magazine about the benefits of exercise and getting fit, she had never really taken much notice. Mary was clearly at the pre-contemplation stage. She didn't see any particular need to change her lifestyle, was aware that facilities were available and that 'exercise was good for you', but none of it really meant anything to her and she saw no reason to do anything differently.

Mary moved to the contemplation stage when she went out to dinner with an old friend who she hadn't seen for some time and who had taken up regular exercise six months before and looked better now than she had in the last six years. Mary's friend was full of enthusiasm for the benefits of regular exercise. She was slimmer, more energetic, looked younger, had clearer skin and seemed more relaxed and less stressed. They had a good dinner and Mary was struck not only by the physical changes in her friend but also the psychological changes. She was also struck by the fact that her friend had the most extravagant pudding on the menu!

At work the next day Mary noticed what she thought was a new poster encouraging staff to have a tryout session at the fitness centre. The poster had actually been there for several weeks but she'd never noticed it before. At this stage Mary didn't do anything different but she became aware that she was reading articles in the paper and magazine about exercise. She watched an interesting TV programme and the subject seemed to come up more frequently in conversations with her friends and colleagues at work. At this stage, Mary was still happy with her current behaviour, still saw no major reason to change but had started thinking about the benefits of regular exercise.

Mary moved into the preparation stage about a month and a half later when she and her family were planning their summer holiday. She thought it would be a good idea to lose a few pounds before the holiday and, as the children wanted to take their bikes on holiday with them, she thought that being a bit fitter meant that they could probably go out cycling for the day as a family. As part of her preparation, Mary went and talked to the fitness centre staff and came away impressed with how easy it was to book an appointment for her first assessment.

Having decided that she was definitely going to exercise regularly, she then started finding reasons not to. She couldn't quite see how she was going to get the time to exercise and, anyway, she didn't have the right clothes. It would have been very easy for Mary to drop out of the change cycle at this stage and continue with her existing behaviours. The bit that made the difference for her is that the fitness centre manager sent her an e-mail following up on her visit and said that he'd arranged for her assessment to take place in four days' time. For Mary the timing was perfect – it was just the trigger she needed to move from preparation to action. The four days gave her chance to buy some clothes and arrange her appointments so that she had time for her assessment.

Mary went for her assessment and was pleased to find that, despite the lack of regular exercise, she was still reasonably fit. She liked the way the fitness centre staff explained her programme and talked positively about the benefits that she should expect to see if she kept to her schedule. Over the next few weeks, Mary maintained her exercise routine. She missed two or three sessions but, on the whole, found it easier to make the change to her lifestyle than she had thought. On the downside, Mary found the exercise quite hard work, she was surprised at how much her muscles ached and how tired she got and she sometimes found it very inconvenient to get to the fitness centre. She'd been told not to expect to see any major changes in her weight and that it would be at least a couple of months before she noticed real improvements in her fitness levels. The staff helped Mary to get through the stage where many people give up exercise because, having done it for a few weeks, they don't see it making any difference and the effort doesn't seem worth while. Mary was also helped by her friends. She found that they were interested in hearing about her fitness routines and encouraged her to keep on going. Her family was also very supportive and made sure she went out for a bike ride every Sunday afternoon.

After about three months of sticking to her exercise routine Mary started to feel the benefits. It was still a struggle to find the time to get along to the fitness centre and making progress was actually harder now than she thought it would be. Fortunately she continued to get support from family and friends, and enjoyed meeting and chatting to people at the fitness centre. There were still times when Mary woke up in the morning and thought that she really couldn't face getting on the treadmill. Times when she found the exercise bike so boring that she just couldn't be bothered with it, but the positives continued to outweigh the negatives and she carried on exercising on a regular basis at least twice and usually three times a week.

Mary gradually found that her posture and muscle tone were better, that she could walk and cycle further, faster and more easily than she could before, and that she felt a lot better. Over the next few months, going to the fitness centre became a regular part of her routine. It wasn't something that she had to think about consciously and she automatically built time into her week to take exercise. She was surprised at how much she missed the fitness centre when she picked up a stomach bug and couldn't exercise for a couple of weeks. It took Mary about a year to move from pre-contemplation through the various stages to termination. The old behaviours where Mary didn't take exercise and didn't see the need for exercise had been replaced, regular routine exercise had become part of her life and there was no suggestion that she might not do it. A year may still be too soon to say that she had truly terminated the old behaviours, and perhaps it would be more precise to regard her as still in the maintenance phase. However, from Mary's point of view she felt that she had achieved lasting behavioural change and no longer considered not exercising.

The Right Messages at the Right Time

Mary's case illustrates the importance of the right messages at the right time. At the pre-contemplation stage, none of the health promotion messages put out by her employer to encourage people to use the fitness centre had any impact on Mary at all. She'd seen them but she hadn't noticed them. She'd heard people talking about the benefits of exercise, read the articles but didn't think they applied to her or were relevant to her situation.

The message that prompted Mary to move into the contemplation stage was a very simple one. Regular exercise improves the way you look, and makes you feel better. The message came from a credible source, her friend, and was delivered with enthusiasm and the implication that taking up exercise could actually be fun. Mary probably wouldn't have taken any notice if her friend's reasons for exercising had been about living longer or running faster. Those things didn't matter to Mary and weren't relevant to her at this stage of her life. Looking good and feeling better were relevant and did matter.

As Mary moved to the contemplation stage, she was exposed to information that helped her decide that taking up exercise was a good thing to do. This information built on and reinforced her reasons for thinking about exercise in the first place and helped move her through the change process. At the preparation stage Mary was helped again. It was easy for her to start exercising and nobody put any barriers in her way. Again, the situation might have been different if she couldn't find out how to start using the fitness centre or if she couldn't find information on joining a local gym. She would have found it difficult to take action if she couldn't make the time to exercise or if her family and the workplace had not been supportive. The key point about the contemplation and preparation stages is that information was available when it was needed and that support was given to encourage her to take action.

Action was easy because the resources that Mary needed to make her behaviour change were available and she was encouraged to make use of them. Starting to exercise wasn't particularly expensive, wasn't massively time-consuming and didn't require a major sacrifice. Other people find that there are far more barriers to taking action. The cost of joining a gym may be expensive, there may not be local facilities, it may not be possible to fit time into home and work schedules. The maintenance stage was also quite straightforward. Perhaps the biggest single benefit Mary had was that she didn't have unrealistic expectations. She wasn't led to believe that she'd lose seven pounds in two weeks or that she'd suddenly be able to run a marathon. The fitness centre staff had carefully managed the benefits that she could expect to get from the exercise and encouraged her to notice small changes in her fitness levels. The monitoring programmes used by the fitness centre helped Mary to see that she was making progress and the continued support and encouragement reinforced the belief that she was doing the right thing. Finally, Mary's attitude changed so that exercise became part of her life. It was no longer something she had to think about and she was helped in this by the understanding that over time it would become easier to exercise than to not exercise and the benefits to her wellbeing, including her physical, psychological and social health, exceeded the cost.

Table 6.1 indicates the kind of messages that need to be given to help people at the various stages of change. As we've seen from our example, there was no point in giving Mary information about different exercise routines when she wasn't even thinking about taking up exercise. Similarly, there is no

Table 6.1

Stages of change	Message content
Pre-contemplation	Motivation
Contemplation	Message information
Preparation	Support
Action	Resource availability
Maintenance	Making progress

point in sending out messages about the support facilities or the type of equipment available in the fitness centre or the wonderful machines for monitoring progress, until people are at the appropriate stage.

The key point is that people need to get the right message at the right time. Organisations face two major difficulties in achieving this goal. The first is that each individual moves through different stages over time and it is difficult to know their current situation. The second is that within an organisation there are people at every stage in the change process. For any specific behaviour change some people will need motivating to consider change, others want the resources to make the change, and so on. The lack of appreciation of stages of change means that organisations don't bother to tailor their messages and, on the whole, don't even bother to think about the impact of their messages on the people whose behaviours they want to change. Health promotion is often therefore 'written off' as a pointless exercise. It won't be if it contains the right messages at the right time, which of course requires you to know a bit more about your employees than most companies do.

THE PERSON-CENTRED APPROACH TO WELLBEING

Workplace Health Programmes

The focus on individual health and the need for the employee to manage their own health is the cornerstone of health promotion programmes. This is the point at which we return to our organisational focus and explore what employers can do to help their people manage their wellbeing. We need to understand how and why people move from wellness to illness and from illness to good health, so that we can encourage and promote positive health behaviours.

Organisations concerned with health at work have, over the years, developed a range of programmes to promote workplace health. These include fitness programmes, weight control programmes, stress management programmes, and so on. Many of these programmes are extremely effective, well thought out, and professionally managed. An individual employee will be invited to take part in one or more of these programmes on the basis of eligibility or a specific health promotion campaign. For example, breast-screening programmes may be made available to women over 35, an executive health medical may be offered to managers who reach a certain grade. Employees may also take part in quit-smoking or weight-loss campaigns as part of company-wide health promotion initiatives. The company does an excellent job of delivering programmes but participation in the programme depends on eligibility, not need. Companies spend enormous sums of money delivering health messages to people who either don't need them or aren't ready for them. We believe that campaigns should target the people at risk or in need. The programmes should be individualistic and highly personalised. It's not the programmes that are important; it's the people.

This involves a change of emphasis from general or 'exclusive' health care programmes to a person-centred approach to the management of workplace health. Start with an understanding of individual needs and then put the programmes in place to improve the health of that individual. Give them the support or assistance they need, at the time they need it and use a method that is appropriate to their circumstances at that time.

Taking this approach reinforces the need to gather information about the health of our employees. It requires us to construct our picture of the 'macro' by starting with the 'micro'. That is to say, there is a need to audit for health at the individual level and then use this information to map the issues on a company-wide level. Many health investments are wasted, as we have seen, because employers make an emotional judgement as to what the issues are likely to be and then seek to involve the employee after the event. Starting with the individual provides an opening for personalised health messages which are linked to issues uncovered via comprehensive health and wellbeing diagnostics supported, if appropriate, by relevant clinical screening. Data collected in this way makes it possible to base wellbeing interventions on the needs of the staff and the organisation, instead of relying on general campaigns that may or may not be relevant.

Product- versus Market-Centred Companies

The situation is analogous to companies that are product rather than market centred. Product-centred businesses start with what they make and try to find customers to buy it. The product may be wonderful, it may do exactly what it's meant to do, be built to high quality, be the right price, be delivered well and so on but, if it's not what people want, then no one will buy it. It's impossible to estimate how many companies have gone out of business because they concentrated on products, not markets.

Companies concerned with changing behaviour can spend millions of pounds on internal communication, managing change events, management training courses, and so on, without thinking about the market for the change programme. They have their product, the change programme, and they're determined to implement it irrespective of the needs of the staff. They fail to analyse the market, their employees, and miss some obvious questions. How much resistance will we meet? How many people want this change? How ready are our people to change? What would make people want to change? Once organisations start thinking this way, the next question is very straightforward: What messages do we need to give at each stage to help people move through the change process? It's then possible to design a change programme that starts with where people are now and identifies the stages that they will need to go through in order to achieve permanent change.

SUMMARY

Wellbeing is an individual issue. The organisation can have a significant influence over health behaviours but it cannot control health or manage health on behalf of the employee. We have seen that the workplace can exacerbate ill health and, often unknowingly, push an employee into illness. We have also seen that problems arising at home can have serious implications for the employer. It is the responsibility of the organisation to encourage good health and, as we have seen in earlier chapters, it is also good business. To be effective these messages have to be tailored to the needs of the individual. The only way this can be achieved is by identifying the issues for each employee and delivering information that is specific, relevant and motivational.

We are all different and we all need to be treated as individuals. One of the most effective ways for organisations to show how much they value their people is to listen to them, to ask them about themselves and, most important of all, to do something with the information. People need to be motivated to change, and different messages are needed at different stages of the change cycle to move them along the path to wellness. When the right messages arrive at the appropriate time, lasting change can occur. A person-centred approach to individual health is a very tangible demonstration of how much the business really cares about its people.

7
Improving the Visible Health Issues – Managing Attendance

MANAGING ATTENDANCE

We identified sickness absence as one of the most visible manifestations of poor wellbeing at work. Unlike some of the other issues we have discussed, individual absence is easy to recognise and, in theory, relatively easy to measure. Unfortunately most organisations find even something as straightforward as absence can be difficult to quantify and manage. Absence data is, in most organisations, notoriously unreliable. Absence frequently goes unrecorded, and where it is captured the reason for the absence is either not known or misrepresented. Worse still, value judgements abound over whether the absence is or is not justified and there is little, if any, follow up. For these companies, absence monitoring is taken to mean the same thing as absence management when in fact they are two completely different activities.

Identifying the true reasons for absence and quantifying the cost of absence tends to be an imprecise activity. Using the reef analogy once more, it is as if spray or mist obscures the rocks standing out of the water. We know they are there, we have a rough idea of the shape and size but we really need to be able to see them more clearly if we are to avoid the danger they represent.

Managing attendance requires clarity of vision and the best possible understanding of the size and nature of the problem.

Many organisations begin the process of managing attendance by trying to quantify the size of the absence problem. They then attempt to discover and classify the reasons for the absence. At this point they realise that it's not as simple as they thought, enthusiasm for the project starts to wane, and they move on to a less difficult problem.

Genuine Illness or Malingering?

Discussions about the reasons for absence usually end up being to do with whether the reason is genuine or not. This quickly brings us to a question of definition. What is a genuine reason for absence? One person's definition of what is a genuine reason for absence will differ from the next. Certainly there are some places where opinion converges. An employee with a slipped disc would be generally be accepted as having a genuine reason for not coming to work. But when can that person return to work? When does the condition cease to become sufficiently non-acute to keep the person off work?

Dr Ann Fingret and Alan Smith, in their book *Occupational Health – A Practical Guide for Managers*, state that sickness absence is 'more realistically termed absence attributed to sickness'. The absence may not always be as a result of genuine sickness. Although it is impossible to be precise about the percentage of absence which is genuinely the result of a medical condition, Fingret and Smith point out that the frequency and length of any absence, for an illness or an injury, are determined by many factors 'other than the actual disease process'. The length of time an individual takes off work as a result of any episode of ill health or accident is therefore a function of personality, availability and suitability of treatment, domestic circumstances and, of course, the nature of the job. Although employers have little involvement in the medical management of the condition, they can influence the other factors.

Individuals suffer from pain and tolerate illness at different degrees depending on their personality and circumstances. The motivation to return to work also varies enormously from person to person. The combination of these two factors will influence how long an individual employee is absent for a specific illness.

An employee with a high tolerance for illness and a strong motivation to return to work will have far less time off work than a colleague with the same illness and the same availability of treatment but low tolerance and low motivation. In both cases the reason for absence is 'genuine'. The effect on the organisation is very different.

Frequently, the distinctions made between genuine and non-genuine reasons for absence are highly judgmental. If you are physically ill, then that is all right; if you are just feeling a little low today, then that is not. 'Non-genuine sickness absences' are thus often more closely aligned to mental health issues than physical ones. However, it is not so easy to make this distinction. To do so means that physical health is given a higher priority than mental wellbeing. This ignores the link between physical and mental ill health and fails to recognise the seriousness of mental health problems.

In any event, to make a distinction between 'genuine' reasons for absence such as physical ill health and 'non-genuine' reasons for absence such as low job dissatisfaction is to miss the point. Whatever the reason for absence, the cost to the company is the same. Any plans to reduce absence should focus on both these areas simultaneously. The emphasis must move away from sickness absence toward managing attendance.

Reasons for Absence are Multifactorial

There have been relatively few studies into the reasons for absence and, up until the early 1970s, most of the research was directed to finding a single cause that could, almost at a stroke, bring about a remedy. More recent studies have stressed that the cause is more likely to be multifactorial, and explanations for differences in absence patterns between groups of employees need to take into account other factors such as personal characteristics, attitudes, values and background. It isn't just the ill or the malingerers that take time off work – motivated and healthy employees also demonstrate absence behaviour. In order to manage attendance we need to understand the reasons why some employees who are physically unwell still come to work, while others who are physically well and highly motivated do not come to work. The most common reason for absence in well and motivated employees is that they are prevented from coming to work because of domestic circumstances. For example, higher absence rates among female employees are not down to poorer health or low levels of job commitment or lack of job satisfaction, but because they frequently carry more of the burden of dealing with child or elder care and domestic problems.

Attendance Motivation

In 'Absence behaviour and attendance motivation: a conceptual synthesis', Nigel Nicholson identifies three main reasons for absence:

- Pain avoidance.
- Adjustment to work.
- Economic decision making.

Nicholson starts from the assumption that attendance is normal behaviour and that most employees attend regularly on 'automatic pilot'. The search for causes of absence should centre on the search for those factors that disturb the normal pattern of attendance. Whether an employee attends in a given set of circumstances depends on a number of variables. The key variables are those that affect 'attachment and attendance motivation', each of which is influenced by a contextual factor. First, the personal characteristics of the individual such as age or gender influence absence. Overlaid onto this are orientations or attitudes to work, which differ according to occupational experience and background. Thirdly, the nature of the job and the opportunities afforded for job satisfaction. A fourth influence arises out of the rules of the workplace that may be either strict or lenient on the absence. The final influence is random and refers to domestic or travel difficulties that may impact on the ability to attend.

Absence Continuum

The result is an absence continuum, ranging from unavoidable influences that impact on frequency of absence to avoidable influences. Nicholson argues that absence control policies should be aimed at tackling avoidable influences. He recognises that these will vary between individuals and work settings, inasmuch as a minor ailment in an older worker involved in heavy manual work will result in a longer absence than the same injury in a younger worker performing light office work. But that seems to be as far as the discussion on the potential impact of ill health goes both in Nicholson's study and in most later variations on the same theme.

This is remarkable because health is surely the single most rewarding *avoidable influence* on absence. But some twenty years on there is still a sense in many companies that absence has little to do with ill health and individual health risk is therefore an unavoidable influence. As we shall see shortly, the common features of most attendance programmes are policy, procedure, reward and punishment. The companies who have wellbeing and disease management programmes at the centre of their attendance management programmes are still few and far between.

The Need for Measurement and the Importance of Monitoring

The traditional approaches to absence management and monitoring are important for two reasons. First, because the collection of good absence data is crucial to the ongoing appraisal of the success of your health care interventions and secondly because it is important that the whole organisation, both employees and their managers, plays a part in obtaining good information about absence. However, we need to emphasise the point that sickness absence is one of the visible manifestations of employee ill health. It is towards the end of the ill health continuum and is therefore, to use a well-known metaphor, about the horse having bolted. Good absence monitoring, however good it is, does not create a healthy workplace. The map is not the territory. Good absence data does however contribute to building the right strategies, provided that the genuine reasons for absence are understood.

What is Good Absence Data and How Do You Get It?

As demonstrated by the 1998 CBI absence and labour turnover survey, some 79% of the sampled organisations have formal procedures for absence reporting and most now make a concerted effort to collect useful data. Increasingly companies are spending time and energy as well as money in developing policy and procedures to improve the quantity and quality of the data produced. Increased focus on the issue has led many to realise that they have 'quantity' in their data but little quality.

As we have already seen, much of this is because the data collected in the past has been used for a different purpose, namely the administration of statutory sick pay. Information abounds on rates of absence but frequently there is little to tell us the reasons why.

So what does good absence data look like and how do we get it? A few points to note are outlined in the following paragraphs.

'Good' Data

Any definition of 'good' in this context must be related to the purpose to which you wish put the data. It can be accurate and it can be complete, but it could still be useless if it does not shed any light on what the employees seem to be saying they have wrong with them. A major part of collecting good data is to ensure that you are capturing the sort of information that will facilitate analysis in the future of both the quantity and the reason for absence. This may sound obvious, but it is the qualitative information about the causes of absence that is frequently missing. This makes the interrogation of absence data as a source of information about what may be 'below the water-line' almost impossible. A good rule of thumb is to try and work through what you would like to know about your absence patterns and then collect the right data items to tell you!

Accuracy—Completeness—Consistency

Another major point is that absence data needs to be both accurate and complete. It is no good having first-class data collected in only 10% of your locations if you want to use the information to try to map health care issues overall. It is often the case that individual divisions or departments within companies can produce very useful data, and this information can be used to better understand what their own unique profile of health issues appear to be. If neighbouring departments or divisions collect different data, or no data at all, then it is risky to project the findings from one part of the company onto others and build a management strategy from there. Likewise it is no good having 100% accuracy in each line of data but only capturing this on 60% of your absences. Therefore it is important to ensure that data is collected throughout the organisation and that what is collected is the same everywhere. Individual managers and departments may want to collect additional information themselves, but there should be a core of information that is mandatory and common to all.

Clear Policy

Absence data is rarely complete or consistent where there is no shared understanding of what the policy and procedures for absence reporting and recording should be. Frequently, when talking to companies about policy and procedures, we have found excellently prepared documentation with workflow diagrams and clearly defined roles and responsibilities for making them a reality. The problem is, nobody follows them.

The first step for most organisations interested in improving the quality of their absence data should be to review the communication and understanding of the procedures currently in place. It may well be that all the existing 'rules' and protocols for reporting and recording absences are sound, but there are currently too many different interpretations as to how they should be followed.

Involvement

Gaining the involvement of employees and managers in recording absences properly will be made much more difficult if there is not a shared understanding of why the monitoring is important. Each employee and every manager needs to accept their part of the responsibility for providing and collecting this type of information.

Achieving this will require two related pieces of work. First, there is a need to explain and educate the entire workforce as to why absence data matters, as well as why and how they will benefit by making their absences known (as well as the real reason for them!). This is clearly going to be very much easier if there is a defined and well-communicated strategy for employee health in place. A clear understanding of the strategy makes it obvious why information gathering is important. Employees are therefore less likely to be suspicious of the policy and will work with it rather than against it. All too often companies overhaul their absence monitoring policies and procedures, usually for the most people friendly of reasons, but the impression gained by the workforce is that this is a new attempt to 'catch them out' rather than help them out.

Considerations of involvement lead us to the eternally thorny question of who is really responsible for absence monitoring? Research carried out in UK companies by the authors would suggest that more often than not human resource personnel believe it to be the responsibility of the line manager, and the line nearly always believe it to be the responsibility of HR. This goes a long way to explaining why there are often so many holes in company absence data!

If, as we know, it is wellbeing issues that keep people from work, then it seems unlikely that HR are the right people to collect the data. Even in the largest HR department there would be insufficient personnel to be close enough to the employees' activities to be able to record what is going on. In companies with the best data, policy is drawn up and communicated by HR, who support the data collection process and manipulate management information to feed back to the line. Responsibility for noticing that the person is off sick sits quite firmly with individual team managers. Ultimately the most effective management of the sickness episode will be achieved through a tripartite relationship between the employee, the line manager and the health or HR professionals, but the initial responsibility rests with the line.

For managers to embrace this involvement they need to fully appreciate both the part they can play in maintaining employee wellbeing and the importance to the organisation of building a healthy workforce. If they do not 'believe' these issues to be important or a legitimate part of their work, then collecting information will be just another exercise in 'red tape'. This message will quickly be communicated to the employees, thus undermining effectiveness all round.

One of the most effective ways of gaining the involvement of managers is to show them how they can use the absence data at a local level to help them manage their team. Once again, very few organisations do this well; they may report on 'absence rates' by department but they don't use the information they collect to help the department run more effectively. For example, managers may become much more interested in absence data if it provides answers to questions such as:

- Should I encourage my staff to have flu jabs? If I pay for the jabs, what effect will it have on reducing my absence levels and what will that save me in time and money?
- One of my administration staff is due to have a hysterectomy. How long is she likely to be away from work? Will she be able to resume her full workload on return or will we need to have a settling-in period?
- I've read that stress is a major problem. What proportion of absence in my department is due, either directly or indirectly, to stress? Is there any evidence that our stress awareness programme reduces stress-related absence?

Good-quality data collection and analysis will provide accurate and relevant answers to these and similar questions based on your organisation's experience of absence. Managers get something in return for taking part in the data collection and, provided that the data is easily accessible, will start to use it in their decision making. Encouraging managers to collect accurate absence data by showing them how it can be used to their benefit is much more effective than trying to impose compliance with procedures that are seen as irrelevant.

What Data to Collect

The answer to this depends very much on what analysis you feel you might want to perform on the data in the future. Too many variables, and the time taken to collect the information becomes prohibitive. Too little data, and it cannot be manipulated to tell you anything about what is really going on.

As a general rule, the following list gives a good spread of variables for both fast 'snapshots' of current trends and flexible multivariate analysis in the future:

- Site identifier.
- Department code.
- Employee number (or some other unique identifier).
- Employee name.
- Start date of illness.
- End date of illness.
- Reason for absence.
- Number of days absence.

You should also collect data on whether or not temporary cover was used during the absence, whether the absence was paid or unpaid, whether the absence was the result of an accident at work, and whether or not the absence was self-certified or a medical certificate was supplied.

The first two of these items assist greatly in calculating the direct cost of absence to the organisation and will therefore provide an easily accessible index against which to quantify the future benefit of reduced absence. Recording absences specifically related to accidents at work will, in addition to providing valuable information for health and safety managers (many of whom feel that a good number of workplace accidents 'slip the net'), provide you with valuable early warnings of potential employee litigation and employer liability exposures. Mapping the patterns and concentrations of these absences will give real risk management information.

Computerised or Manual Records?

Prior to 1997, CBI absence surveys seemed to show that companies with computerised absence recording experienced lower rates of absence. There may have been a number of reasons for this, among them that those with data fields to fill are more likely to have formal absence monitoring procedures which create a sentinel effect.

Interestingly, in the 1997 CBI survey it was the companies with manual recording systems who were now reporting lower levels of absence; an average of 7.4 days per employee as against

8.9 in companies keeping computer records and 8.5 days in companies keeping a mixture of the two. However, the high number of smaller companies in that particular year's survey probably explains this. Smaller companies are generally known to experience a lower number of average days lost through sickness.

There is no doubt that if the right data is collected in the first place, computer-based records will make subsequent data analysis easier, faster and much more powerful. But remember that the existence of a computerised system for measurement does not guarantee good data. As was so memorably put by one HR system provider at a recent conference, if the policy and procedures are not right then it will be 'rubbish in, rubbish out, only now it will be faster and in colour!'. If your company is about to invest in new technology to capture absence data, then one of the overriding considerations should be the capacity it has to link with other sources of information about your people. As we said in Chapter 5, being able to link diverse data covering all aspects of employee wellbeing can be of enormous benefit when it comes to analysing causal relationships. Even if the immediate requirement is for a stand-alone system, the potential for future data integration should not be ignored.

Reason for Absence Coding

One of the most important facets of data collection is the necessity for accurate and consistent coding of the reason for absence. This is frequently the piece of data that is the most badly recorded or missing altogether. As a result, much of what is currently collected in UK companies is of limited use for the purpose of understanding underlying wellbeing issues.

In planning how to capture this information, there are a number of points to consider. The first and most important is that the reasons for absence should be captured using a finite set of codes. Data is collected in order to facilitate analysis and little analysis can be performed on a list of narrative reasons. Secondly, there needs to be a standardised set of reasons from which all personnel tasked with capturing data must choose from. This means that the information can easily be categorised and the categories compared across the organisation. There are several 'standard' coding systems such as the READ codes and the ICD codes that provide a structured categorisation of illness that can be used to benchmark absence both within and outside the organisation.

We have seen coding systems that range from a list of as little as five reasons, which is so small that in this company absences related to heart disease are consolidated with absences for flu, to one with nearly 300 different codes. This one, much more incisive when it comes to analysis, obviously has its problems since it is potentially too unwieldy to use. The balance is somewhere between 40 for a manual system and 100–150 for a computerised system. The latter has the advantage of being able to store absence codes 'behind' one another, so that the first list of absence reasons to be offered can be ones covering the most common complaints. If none of these fits the circumstances, the next menu can contain the same reasons but further subdivided to provide more detailed options and so on.

Not all absences will fall neatly into the reason codes that a company has settled on. 'Virus' is too broad a category to be much help later on in data analysis, but frequently that is all the employee knows because it is all their GP has told them. Similarly, not all employees will give the real reason anyway, so there will always be a slight risk of coding error. The point is that most employees do know what their health issues are and most will supply the information if asked in the right way. It seems a shame not to ask them. Too often the potential for miscoding is used as the reason why there is no point in trying to get it right the other 85% of the time. It is obviously better to have 85% of the information right than none at all.

While still on the subject of coding, 'other' and 'unknown' must be banned. Once this category is available in a coding schedule you can almost guarantee that the quality of your reason coding will take a sharp turn for the worse. In most cases we have seen that removing 'other' and 'unknown' as options has dramatically improved the quality of the data by encouraging line managers to talk to the employee in order to find out why they were away from work.

Collecting good qualitative information about the reason for absence is key to getting robust absence data. Without it, it is difficult to see what the data is telling you in terms of what the health issues might be and how to intervene. If you have no clue about why the employee is way from work, the opportunity for appropriate case management and support for them during their illness is substantially reduced. At a company-wide level you will be unable to use the data to give you insights into overall risk and where opportunities lie to mitigate those risks and attendant costs. It is also very difficult to link the data to any other employee wellbeing information.

A good example of how this can work is in a company that analysed the data they had been collecting on the costs associated with employees receiving physiotherapy for musculoskeletal problems. On its own the data did not mean very much, but when the information was cross-correlated with their absence data, the picture became very much more interesting. The company's absence data contained good information about the reasons for absence, and by linking the two data sets it was possible to see a clustering of absences for back and knee injuries that directly matched data they possessed on claims for outpatient treatment. On further investigation it became apparent that many of those affected were involved in manual lifting and so it was now possible to calculate the broader costs associated with those absences. More importantly, it gave the company some very valuable information about where to focus their manual handling advice by way of proactive intervention.

Medical Certificates

Asking for medical certificates normally features in most UK sickness absence policy and procedures, but their reliability as a source of information for monitoring the reasons for absence is open to debate. In the UK, a medical certificate is usually required before statutory sick pay or occupational sick pay is paid. For short-term absence, most employers insist on self-certification. This requires the employee to complete and sign a form stating the reason for their absence. Periods of illness that last longer than seven days are usually supported by a medical certificate, usually but not always signed by the employee's doctor. Although there are a few notable exceptions, it's very unusual for an employee's doctor not to provide a medical certificate. If an employee complains of feeling run down or suffering from back pain, stomach upsets, etc., most doctors find it hard to refuse to accept their symptoms. Even so, there have been some amusing examples of doctors being somewhat sceptical about the nature of the illness and giving the reason for illness as 'ergophobia', i.e. fear of work or, in another example, oscillatus plumbus (swinging the lead). However, these examples are rare and the vast majority of medical certificates appear to offer genuine reasons for absence.

Perhaps the most common misrepresentation concerns the avoidance of stress or other mental ill health issues as a reason for absence. The stigma attached to mental ill health is still so strong that doctors list the physical symptoms rather than mention the underlying illness. In organisations where mental ill health and stress are regarded as weaknesses, this will not be given as a reason for absence on a self-certification form. It will also not be given on a doctor's medical certificate. When faced with an employee who is genuinely worried that their depression, anxiety or stress may adversely affect their employment prospects, most doctors would be willing to label the illness with one of the physical symptoms of stress, such as stomach upsets, exhaustion, flu, etc.

As we have already argued, cases of people malingering are relatively infrequent. In organisations with a culture of 'sickies', where people regularly take time off work and claim that they are sick, the employer should recognise this as a deep-rooted problem with attitude, values and motivation that needs to be addressed at source. The working environment is also a major factor in determining an individual employee's willingness to return to work after genuine illness. If the employee finds the workplace supportive and encouraging, and the work fulfilling, he will be eager to return to work and persuade the doctor that he is capable of taking up his duties. An employee who doesn't find work fulfilling, who isn't valued by her employer, who doesn't gain support from her fellow workers will, on the other hand, take every opportunity to extend her time off work. In all probability she will seek to persuade the doctor that she hasn't fully recovered, that the duties she has to undertake are physically demanding and so on.

Return-to-Work Interviews

The problems with self-certified or medically certified absence can, to a large extent, be overcome by properly conducted return-to-work interviews. Similarly, much of the difficulty surrounding the appropriate coding of absences for recording purposes can be overcome by a sensitively conducted interview with the employee when they return to work. These interviews can be held face to face or, if more convenient or for shorter absences, over the phone.

As well as providing more accurate information about the nature of illness, the return-to-work interviews have also been found to act as a powerful deterrent to unauthorised absence. However, care must be taken. Some organisations make the return-to-work interview a humiliating experience, during which the employee is made to feel guilty for having taken time off and effectively given the third degree about the real reason for their absence. This is likely to result in poor information, less honesty and a misrepresentation of the real reasons for absence. Don't try to combine information gathering with policing absence, it won't work.

Organisations need to have clear guidelines and train their managers and human resource people in how to conduct return-to-work interviews. It's essential to get the balance right. A properly conducted return-to-work interview can demonstrate the employer's concern for the employee's wellbeing. The interview demonstrates that the employee is valued and that it's good they are back at work. It also gives the employer the opportunity to check that the employee is well enough to manage their duties and to identify any support that may be required. The vast majority of employees want to get back to work and have no need of any particular help or assistance. For these people, the return-to-work interview is a fairly straightforward process. However, in situations where the illness has been more severe or the work environment is particularly demanding, the return-to-work interviews should not be skimped. A few individuals will need help in making an effective and speedy return to work. They may need to work restricted hours, or take time for visits to doctors, physiotherapists or other rehabilitation specialists. If the job involves physical effort, they may need to be put on lighter work or given clear instructions on manual handling.

Failure of the Return-to-Work Interview

If the employer makes a commitment to the employee at the return-to-work interview, it is essential that it is fulfilled. In the UK, the celebrated case of a Local Government Social Services Manager, illustrates the dangers of not fulfilling an agreed course of action. The manager had a particularly demanding job working in the child abuse section of Social Services. He had a nervous breakdown and was off work for a long period. He recovered and on his return to work his employer undertook to provide him with more support and a reduced caseload. Although this was the case for the first few weeks after returning to work, the situation quickly deteriorated and the manager was left without the support he had been promised. The pressures grew and he once again suffered a nervous breakdown. He brought a case against his employer for compensation in respect of stress at work and received an out-of-court settlement reported to be around £175 000.

The implication for employers is very clear. When someone returns to work and the return-to-work interview establishes that they need help and assistance, that obligation must be met. It isn't good enough to go through the motions, pay lip service to the needs of the employee and then carry on doing what you've always done.

Trigger Points

Trigger points are predefined points at which a pattern of absence becomes eligible for further investigation. They are an increasingly common part of absence and attendance policy in many UK companies. Sadly, the motivation for this procedure is sometimes geared towards catching the malingerers rather than seeking an early warning that there may be wellbeing problems. That said, the principle is sound and certainly the right practice of defining what the trigger points should be, and following up with sickness counselling, can act as a fine mesh in which to catch those who may need help.

Different organisations calculate and set trigger points at different levels. Some examples follow.

Example 1. Local government

The employee is involved in a formal review of absence when he or she, over a three-month period, reaches any of the following thresholds:

- Three periods of uncertified absence.
- Three periods of self-certified absence.
- Three periods of medically certified absences exceeding 7 days.
- A combination of the above on at least three occasions.
- Unacceptable patterns of absence, e.g. regular Monday or Friday absences.

Example 2. Manufacturing

- Single absences of 28 calendar days or more.
- A total of 4 days' certified or non-certified absence in multiple spells over a rolling 12-month period.
- More than 3 episodes of absence in a 6-month rolling period.
- On reporting any condition that may indicate a significant illness or incapacity, e.g.
  - disease of the heart or blood vessels;
  - recurrent anxiety, depression or other mental disorder;
  - recurrent back problems;
  - serious infectious diseases;
  - persistent skin disorder;
  - major injury or operation;
  - diabetes;
  - epilepsy, fits or blackouts;
  - disorders associated with pregnancy;
  - WRULD/RSI/tenosynovitis;
  - a sustained drop in performance or significant behaviour or personality change.

Example 3. The Bradford factor

Developed at the University of Bradford, this system has been adopted by a number of organisations. It is a formula that measures individual employee absence by giving more weight to frequent short-term absences. This is in recognition that frequent short-term absences are more disruptive than isolated longer spells. It is the accumulation of 'points' that triggers review.

The system uses an absence rating indicator, $S \times S \times H$, where S = the number of incidences of absence over a 52-week period, and H = the total number of absent hours over the period.

Using this method it is possible to see how different patterns of absence accumulate points:

An individual with two periods of absence totalling 10 days (80 hours using an 8-hour day) would be rated at $2 \times 2 \times 80 = 320$ points.

An individual with six periods of absence totalling 10 days (80 hours) would be rated at $6 \times 6 \times 80 = 2880$ points.

Organisations who have adopted this approach set what they believe to be the appropriate level of points to act as the 'trigger' for further intervention.

Certain types of absence are usually excluded from the calculations, namely absence due to work-related injury, accidents, or absence due to a pregnancy-related illness and absence due to serious progressive illness.

It is also possible for the employee to recover a clean absence record, usually by demonstrating a predefined period of continuous attendance.

Sickness Counselling

Often the next stage for those organisations that either formally or informally use trigger points to commence interventions, sickness counselling is a valuable opportunity to find out more about the health issues faced by the employee. In one NHS environment, anyone with four occasions or episodes of sickness absence receives formal sickness counselling.

As with return-to-work interviews, these meetings need to be conducted sensitively if they are not to be counter-productive. The vast majority of employees concerned will be genuinely unwell and it is vital that they are not left feeling interrogated, doubted or guilty about being ill.

STRATEGIES FOR MANAGING ATTENDANCE

The Influence of Peer Pressure

Work group or peer pressure may influence attendance patterns either way; it can either encourage attendance or it can encourage absence. Which of these two applies in your organisation is an indicator of whether you have an absence culture or an attendance culture.

Companies have recognised the link between peer pressure and absence rates and have sought to harness the power of peer group pressure to control absence. The 'big stick' approach to managing absence through peer group pressure can be extremely effective in the short term. A small, £10 million turnover, engineering company based in the North of England provides a good example of the dangers of using peer group pressure to control absence. The business employed 100 people and was run by two men who had grown their business from a small welding shop. The company was typical of many small engineering firms; their factory was on an industrial estate on the outskirts of town, and the working environment was dirty, noisy and a bit chaotic. The workforce was predominantly male and the majority were skilled welders.

Although the company was successful and had good long-term contracts, they had a massive problem in meeting delivery dates. They were continually letting their customers down and jeopardising their business as a result. One of the reasons for poor delivery was the extremely high absence levels. Most weeks, over 25% of the workforce would miss at least one day, usually a Friday. The company compensated by introducing compulsory overtime, but this simply increased costs and absence rates increased further, cancelling out the effect of overtime working. The company made a classic mistake of dealing with the symptom, not the source of the problem.

They decided that the best way to reduce absenteeism was to penalise the workers by taking money out of their wage packet. For the first couple of weeks after introducing financial penalties the absence levels dropped, but then started shooting up again. Quite simply, the workforce had realised that they could earn more in overtime than they lost by being penalised for absence. The company then decided to use peer group pressure. They introduced a scheme that effectively reduced everyone's wages if anyone was absent even for one day, irrespective of the reason for absence. This created an atmosphere where people were simply afraid to have time off work. It was a tough, macho working environment and after the first couple of absences had been 'dealt with' by fellow workers, the company started getting almost 100% attendance.

Unfortunately, and as might be expected, this did not solve the delivery problems. Things seemed to take longer to get through the factory, jobs weren't finished in time and, even worse, quality took a massive downturn. The company operated an old-fashioned quality control system, with inspectors checking finished parts. The number of rejects increased dramatically and the company was in a worse state than before.

Over the next few months, the company continued struggling with quality issues, poor performance and lack of productivity, and started to notice other things going wrong. Despite the penalties, absence was once again becoming an issue and some of the best workers were leaving. The company's reputation as a tough employer had spread around the town and they were finding it increasingly difficult to recruit replacements. A year after 'solving' their absence problem, the company went bust.

The punishment-based strategies we have described were effective in reducing absence in the short to medium term but had no long-term benefit. They reduced employee wellbeing and serve as an excellent illustration of the dangers of the reef. The company avoided the visible danger, only to be ripped apart by the hidden issues of dissatisfaction and alienation

Attendance Incentives

A more acceptable approach to managing attendance is the payment of attendance bonuses. Employees are rewarded for coming to work, by participating in some form of bonus scheme. This can be based on collective attendance, where every employee receives a bonus if overall attendance is at the target level, or on individual attendance. A number of schemes combine the collective and individual approach, so that eligibility for a bonus depends on both the overall target and individual attendance.

As well as schemes offering a cash bonus, there are many incentive programmes designed to reward good attendance. These include vouchers, air miles or being eligible for entry into a prize draw.

The Use of Penalties or Rewards to Manage Attendance

The 1997 CBI survey reports that the percentage of companies operating policies of attendance bonuses, waiting days before occupational sick pay is payable, and using absence records as a determinant of redundancy, have all doubled in the last three years. Interestingly, these three policies were ranked bottom in terms of their effectiveness by the companies taking part in the survey, but still there is a growth in their use.

In our experience, attendance bonuses or penalty schemes deal with the symptoms not the causes of absence. Organisations shouldn't need to give people extra incentives to encourage them to come to work. The vast majority of people without jobs would rather be working than unemployed. However, our research shows that only 60% of employees believe that work improves the quality of their lives. As we spend such a high proportion of our waking hours at work it seems reasonable to expect that work should add to, not detract from, our quality of life. We believe that far more people would look forward to work, and would not need additional financial incentives to attend, if more attention was given to making the workplace more satisfying and fulfilling so that it added to the quality of life.

Organisations that penalise absence have an even greater problem. They concentrate their efforts on forcing people to come to work and fail to appreciate the damaging effects of presenteeism. If they understood the true cost of poor employee wellbeing, they would realise that policing absence saves pennies but costs pounds. It would be more productive in the long term if the effort that went into designing and administering compliance schemes was redirected toward understanding and rectifying the underlying causes of absence.

Presenteeism

The problems with the 'stick' approach to managing attendance are highlighted by the growing concern about presenteeism. Presenteeism is a new way of talking about pressure to attend. It describes a situation in which people come to work even though they shouldn't. They are present in body but not in mind. It is generally seen as a feature of times of economic uncertainty, when a poor attendance record could be enough to put someone on the redundancy list. Presenteeism is often driven by the fear of losing a job or of being passed over for promotion. Now it is not so much a question of job loss, but of the consequences of not being present when other people are. In a working culture where long hours equals high commitment, being absent can seriously damage your career. Many people, particularly the ambitious or the high fliers, don't need rules or policies to keep them at work even though they are ill. Their drive and the company culture provide the impetus to attend.

The problem with presenteeism is that it distorts the picture of health revealed by careful analysis of attendance data. We assume that low levels of absence are indicators of good wellbeing, but we know that this is not always the case. We have seen organisations, like the welding company mentioned above, which proudly point to their almost 100% attendance levels. We have also walked around these companies and felt the low morale, noticed the lack of involvement and seen the accident statistics. These are companies where presenteeism is rife. It is the new industrial disease and it is causing serious damage to people and their organisations. This is why absence data should be used with care. Does fear or commitment drive attendance? We need to take other factors into consideration and look at the broader picture to find the answer.

Peer Group Pressure to be Absent

We have looked at the way organisations can apply pressure to encourage staff to attend, but peer group pressure can also work the other way and create an absence culture. There is a belief held by some employers that 'others getting away with absence' is one of the major causes of absence. These employers believe that people take time off work not because they are ill, but because that's what other people do. This attitude is symptomatic of deep-seated organisational malaise. It indicates serious problems with morale and with management style. 'Getting away with absence' implies that the absence is spurious – it suggests that the employee is taking advantage of the employer and that, when other employees see this happening, they will take time off as well. If they don't, they're missing out. The attitude is predicated on an assumption that the workplace is a battleground between workers and management. It is an 'us and them' world in which workers try to do as little as possible and managers have to force them to work. In this world the workers gain some advantage when they get away with absence, managers win when they succeed in stopping them. Health and wellbeing are irrelevant, it's winning or losing that matters.

This attitude is an extreme example of the confrontational approach to sickness absence; it typifies an absence culture in which managers regard absence as a failure in the battle to control the workplace and the employees see sickness as the opportunity to gain a few days of additional holiday. Absence levels are managed by strengthening the policing of absence, by tightening up the rules and, in effect, forcing people to stay at work.

There is evidence to suggest that this is the approach taken by a large number of employers. For some of the more macho firms, perhaps in the engineering or construction industries, their organisational culture and values make it predictable that this line would be taken. But surprisingly the same approach can also be found in the caring professions, as in the following example.

Joanna, a nurse in a major UK teaching hospital, was describing the pressures that she and her colleagues face and the hospital's attitude toward absence management. In Joanna's hospital the nurses are allowed two episodes of sickness absence per annum. If they go one day over their 'allocation' they are given a warning. One further absence after that and they are dismissed. This policy seems designed to place enormous pressure on the nurses not to get ill in the first place, despite the fact that the chances of their health being affected by their work must be greater than in many other occupations. The nurses work in an environment where constant staff shortages coupled with insufficient resources combine to increase further the degree of difficulty associated with the job. A job which already involves long hours, low pay and labour which is both emotionally and physically demanding.

The hospital's policy seems counter-productive for many reasons. In our experience the 'brickbats' approach to absence management rarely produces long-term benefits, because the fear, ill will and lowered morale that are attendant with feeling you are unable to admit to being ill damages the organisation in other ways. It seems particularly inappropriate in this example because, as Joanna said, 'You do not do this job for the money, you do it because you want to'. Malingerers are therefore likely to be rare and it seems pointless to develop an absence policy designed to catch out behaviour that in all probability is not there. Why make life difficult for caring and committed employees as a result of a policy designed to prevent behaviours that are unlikely to occur. It is significant that when Joanna described the hospital's policy she was not actually complaining about the rules, she just accepted, with an air of resignation, that this is the way it is.

Sick Pay Schemes Protect Earnings

Another example of the confrontational approach to absence is the view that people take time off because their sick pay schemes protect their earnings. The assumption behind this view is that it is the threat of loss of earnings that keeps people at work. If organisations stopped sick pay, sickness absence levels would be significantly reduced. This may have a short-term impact but is unlikely to produce lasting change. Evidence for the relationship between absence levels and sick pay usually comes from organisations that have introduced sick pay schemes, giving additional benefits to employees rather than taking them away. In these organisations, absence levels do increase for a few months after introducing the sick pay scheme, but then return to previous levels. Cynical employers may also believe that the employee's GP adds to the problem, presumably by 'signing off' the employee whether or not their illness is genuine.

These factors – others getting away with absence, sick pay

schemes and supportive doctors – combine to reinforce the belief held by many managers that absence is due to malingering. The employee, aided and abetted by his GP, takes every opportunity to abuse the system and, if this is the case, the traditional management view is quite straightforward: 'Don't let people get away with it', penalise individuals for taking time off work and disbelieve what the doctors tell you.

In contrast, issues such as increased pressure on the individual at work, poor quality in working life, lack of control, autocratic management styles, erratic inconsistent management, etc., point to absence as the outcome of poor people management. These reasons for absence create a very different picture from the 'getting away with it' mentality. They describe an environment where the reasons for absence are a function of management style not employee attitude. In this environment, managing sickness absence involves changing culture and management style to enhance employee wellbeing.

Us and Them Attitudes

We believe that these two, apparently diametrically opposed, views on the reasons for absence are in fact two sides of the same story. Our work in a wide range of organisations demonstrates over and over again that when the working environment is bad, when managers are autocratic and inconsistent and don't value the people that work in the business, then an 'us and them' attitude is the order of the day. Employees respond to the lack of control and influence, poor communication, increased pressures and lack of appreciation by 'playing the system'. In workplaces where there is no trust between managers and their staff, everyone plays a zero sum game. If the employees 'get away with something', management lose. If management 'get away with something', employees lose. There is no working towards mutually beneficial goals and creating win-win situations. In this environment it's not surprising that employees will try to 'get away with absence' or work below their level of ability. People who, in the rest of their lives, are honest, trustworthy individuals, will from time to time take advantage of a system that they see as unfair.

The irony is that this situation becomes self-fulfilling. In organisations where management and workers are in opposition it's not surprising that managers believe that 'absence has to be controlled'. On the surface, this attitude appears to produce acceptable results. Employers who adopt draconian methods of policing and controlling sickness absence can report very low absence rates and congratulate themselves on sorting out the problem. These organisations seem to miss the point that perhaps the culture and management styles created the problem in the first place and that by policing absence they are simply managing the symptoms, the visible signs, without addressing the fundamental problem.

Unfortunately, few companies have really started to manage employees' health with the same amount of fervour and enthusiasm as the companies that police absence. Yet the rewards flowing from this approach will be manifestly higher than the savings from reduced occupational sick pay and the marginal improvement in absence rates that will flow from catching out a few more 'malingerers'.

SUMMARY

Employee absence is one of the most visible indicators of poor wellbeing — it is the biggest outcrop on the reef. But even though it can be seen for miles, the detail is usually obscured. We get some idea of what the reef looks like, but it's hard to tell what it's made of and it will almost certainly be much bigger than we think. It is also connected to other parts of the reef that are hidden from view, but are nevertheless a source of danger.

To manage absence we need to shift our approach and focus on managing attendance. We need to make it easy for people to come to work and we shouldn't need to find artificial ways of rewarding or penalising them based on the number of days they are absent. When they are absent we should seek ways to support them and help them get back to work. We need to be careful in the use of attendance management data and recognise that it has to be interpreted in the light of company policies that may encourage presenteeism and misrepresent the true level of employee wellbeing. Most importantly, we should focus on the *causes* of absence and deal with the underlying issues of health and wellbeing that prevent people coming to work. Helping them when they are ill is important, and for some companies it may be the place to start, but it is not the same as managing absence by stopping them becoming unwell in the first place.

8

Improving the Hidden Health Issues

We have argued throughout this book that employee health and wellbeing is an integral component of organisational effectiveness. People are the organisation and their contribution to organisational success is influenced by the way they are treated. Improving employee wellbeing is not a superficial issue, it is the legitimate concern of every manager and supervisor in the business. We have seen how difficult it can be to measure the true cost of employee health and how the major problems are hidden below the surface, with the visible manifestations such as absence levels or staff turnover being a very small part of the overall cost. Paying attention to the surface issues focuses on the symptoms of ill health, whereas going below the surface reveals the real issues and places the emphasis on the causes of poor wellbeing. Organisations that wish to improve wellbeing at work should focus their efforts on the sources as well as the symptoms.

WELLBEING

Work is a holistic experience. Everything that happens at work, or is associated with work, affects employee wellbeing either positively or negatively. In most cases the factors that reduce wellbeing are different from the factors that promote wellbeing, so people at work can be simultaneously motivated and demotivated. For example, they can be motivated by the work itself but demotivated by the way they are managed: 'If only they'd just let me get on with my work' is a commonly heard comment. It is the interrelationship between the various aspects of work that makes understanding wellbeing so difficult. We saw in Chapter 5 that it is possible to model the wellbeing dynamics of the workplace and identify factors that either promote good wellbeing or make people ill.

The key point is that it isn't just one issue. Wellbeing is driven by a complex interplay of issues, with some having a positive influence and others a negative influence. Statistical modelling shows us that the issues are not interchangeable. You can't solve a problem in management style by improving the performance management system. In order to break through the complexity we need to focus attention on specific issues. We should isolate various elements of the experience of work, examine their impact on wellbeing and design appropriate interventions. We must not, however, forget that wellbeing is driven by the interplay between these elements as well as the elements themselves.

In developing strategies for improving wellbeing at work we need to recognise that we can't do everything at once. We need to focus on one or two issues that have a significant influence on the outcomes we need to change. We may also wish to focus on issues that influence many different outcomes, as supportive leadership did in the example described in Chapter 5. Because every aspect of work has an influence on wellbeing, the list of possible factors would be endless. The following factors are a starting point, prompts for identifying possible interventions that will have a positive impact on employee wellbeing:

- Work environment.
- Management style.
- Recruitment and selection processes.
- Communications.
- Induction.
- Job design.
- Performance management.
- Flexible working.
- Values.

- Remuneration.
- Influence and job discretion.
- Career progression.
- Training and development.
- Family-friendly policies.
- Wellness programmes.
- Workplace support.
- Team development.
- Supportive leadership.
- Flexible working practices.
- Good equipment (particularly in high tech organisations).
- Positive reinforcement.
- Organisational affinity and pride.
- Business success.

When we look at the above list, we can see that factors operate at different levels. Some are straightforward procedural issues that really should be developed as comprehensively as possible. This includes recruitment and selection policies, family-friendly policies, performance management systems and so on. Others, such as positive reinforcement, clear and open communications, and supportive leadership, are aspects of management and organisational style that need to be developed and enhanced. Others such as organisational affinity and value matching go to the heart of the relationship between the employee and the employer and underlie other factors on the list.

Each organisation will have its own set of issues that influence workplace wellbeing. Although some factors will be common to many organisations, each business will have its own signature of wellbeing. The above items are a checklist of factors that should be considered when trying to identify the drivers for workplace wellbeing.

There is a wealth of information published about each of the issues in the above list, and the Bibliography at the end of the book makes recommendations for further reading. For the rest of this chapter we will highlight a few of the most useful areas for intervention and make the link to wellbeing more explicit. We recognise that in order to improve wellbeing at work we need to get the basics right. We have seen that although our intent is to improve all aspects of workplace wellbeing, it's easier to start with those issues that have the most influence on the visible health issues, particularly attendance and staff turnover.

Working Environment

Let us begin with the basics. The working environment is the foundation stone of a healthy workplace. People should work in conditions that are safe, pleasant, comfortable and designed to support the tasks that people perform. Above and beyond the basic environmental needs, the workplace should promote self-esteem and physically demonstrate that employees matter. For example, some workplaces are clean, safe and reasonably pleasant, but they look as if the employees have been put in as an afterthought. They have to work in cramped or uncomfortable surroundings, and spend every day struggling with office equipment or machinery that has been installed without regard for how people will use it. Many manufacturing plants are designed to optimise process flow, and equipment is laid out without any regard for the needs of the workers. The employees are expected to adjust to, or put up with, the physical conditions dictated by the machines when, with a little more thought, the environment could have been optimised for people and process. The design of the workplace is about the value of people as well as ergonomics. In a healthy workplace, the machines should work for the people, not the other way round.

We also see this imbalance between people and equipment in offices. Although we have moved away from the 1950s environment of long rows of desks to a more informal layout, many offices still put design considerations before people. For example, some organisations spend millions of pounds on office furniture and carefully designed interiors without allowing for any expression of individuality. One highly profitable manu-facturing company created a new state-of-the-art office environ-ment with the latest in expensive modular furniture but dismayed their employees by placing the desks in neat formations, each at 90 degrees to the other. The designers couldn't understand why people reacted so unfavourably to the new offices and the facilities manager fought a losing battle to prevent staff from rearranging the furniture to a less formal pattern.

At the other extreme, an increasing number of organisations have successfully moved away from the traditional office layout. They have created working environments where people can express their individuality, can lay the space out to suit their needs and encourage open communication rather than being governed by an overriding 'design' concept. One factor driving the reorganisation of office space is the need for people to come together in informal or flexible workgroups. These organisations, operating mainly in the 'creative' or service industries such as advertising, pull people together in small project teams or for specific accounts. They work together in informally arranged areas, making use of equipment, floor area and wall space as appropriate to the task. The new generation of telephones and notebook computers allow people to be contacted wherever they are in the building or at any of the locations. Work has, for far too many people, come to mean the place they go to, not the jobs they do. A healthy work environment recognises that flexibility in the workplace operates both ways. In means that employees should be flexible in their work arrangements so that they come together to meet the needs of the organisation, and organisations should be flexible in the way staff use space and time to get the job done.

Management Style

Our work with organisations has shown that management style, the way people are managed, is one of the most significant factors in employee wellbeing. Being a bad manager, like being a bad lover or a bad driver, is not something that people will readily admit and yet very few people really manage their people well. Countless books have been written on management style and the secrets of good management. Writers like Ken Blanchard have distilled some excellent basic principles into short, easy-to-follow books, like the *One-Minute Manager Series*. Our experience shows that good management is built on respect for the individual and the ability to communicate and motivate toward a common vision. Respect is an old-fashioned word that goes to the heart of management style. The worst managers are the ones with no respect for the people who work for them, who don't value them as individuals and treat people as objects or units of production who exist only to be used to further the manager's objectives. Lack of respect underlies some of the worst manifestations of bad management such as bullying, harassment, discrimination and intimidation. Respect for others should be the cornerstone of all management training, yet it is rarely seen on the prospectus and isn't a quality that's usually explored in selection interview.

Respect, although necessary, isn't sufficient for good management. Many people fail to make good managers because they don't have a clear understanding of what they're trying to achieve or, if they do, are unable to communicate this to their staff. Often, managers make things worse by pretending to know what's going on, even if they don't. We call this the myth of managerial infallibility. Managers are not allowed not to know what's going on. They feel obliged to pretend that they have information, are part of the plan, even when they have been excluded from the decision making and implementation process. As a result, their staff feel that information is being withheld, that knowledge is not being shared and, ultimately, that the staff aren't important enough to need to know.

We have seen the damage caused by a failure to admit that managers don't know what's going on in countless organisations. The situation is particularly acute during times of change or reorganisation. The staff almost always believe that managers know more than they do and information is being deliberately withheld. As a result, they feel devalued, that they can't be trusted with confidential information or that they are not important enough to matter Whatever the reason, the feelings are the same: low morale, suspicion, lack of trust. In the absence of 'official' information, the rumour mill takes over. Nature abhors a vacuum and an information vacuum is quickly filled with whatever debris is floating around the organisation. Because of the perceived lack of trust, the rumours will almost certainly be negative rather than positive and damage both the employee and the business. Even in times of relative stability, a lack of information or badly communicated messages can be highly detrimental. The solution is easy. Talk to people on a regular basis. Let them ask questions, answer honestly and openly. If something is confidential and cannot be shared, then say so. And say why. People will accept that there are sensitive decisions to be made, confidences to be kept. They cannot accept that they cannot be trusted.

Communication

It is difficult to separate communication from management style. The two clearly go hand in hand and, as we have already discussed, the way in which a manager communicates with staff is a key determinant not only of employee wellbeing but also, we believe, of organisational effectiveness. Good communication should be a characteristic of the whole organisation and it is a much broader issue than the relationships between managers and the people that work for them. Communications are about the way that information flows within the organisation and between the organisation and the outside world. Good communication lies at the heart of organisational effectiveness and of employee wellbeing. It is based on respect, understanding, and the willingness to share information and ideas freely and without fear of ridicule or recrimination. People should be encouraged to talk openly and honestly with anyone in the organisation about issues that matter to them or are relevant to their work. The antithesis of good communication is the belief that knowledge is power and people should only have access to information that they 'need to know'. It is very difficult to make people feel valued and involved if they are kept in the dark.

It needs to be recognised that open and informal communication is about more than sharing information. It depends on the ability to listen and an appreciation of the need to respect other people's time. As always, there is a fine line between too much and too little communication and many people make the mistake of thinking that, where communication is concerned, it's the amount that matters. A large public utility made this mistake when they introduced a major programme designed to improve internal communications. Some time after this programme was introduced we were asked to help the managers to identify the factors that were causing stress among their employees. Stress was known to be an issue and there was evidence to suggest it was getting worse. When they were presented with the results of the survey, the senior managers were surprised to find that poor communications was a major contributor to low morale.

As part of the communications programme all the managers had been trained in communication skills and the company had invested considerable time and money in new communications technology and training to support this technology. The senior managers had acted with the best intentions, but failed to realise that in trying to improve communications they had gone from too little to too much. Our research showed that the employees in this organisation felt overwhelmed by the amount of information they had to absorb. They simply couldn't cope with the volume. Managers were copying almost every piece of information to everybody, e-mails flooded the IT system and staff briefings took up so much time for so little benefit that they had become something to be avoided at all costs. The business had missed the key point about improving communications – it's the quality of communication that matters, not the quantity.

Respect for the individual is another major contributor to employee wellbeing. Acting with honesty and integrity is critical. It is difficult to have good communications in an organisation that is characterised by fear, mistrust and manipulation. It's also important to be consistent in the way that you communicate with people, both within and outside the organisation. It's hard for employees to believe that they're being treated fairly and honestly if they are encouraged to lie to their customers or deceive their suppliers.

Reward and Recognition

Interwoven with management style and communication is the way in which people's contributions are recognised and rewarded in an organisation. It is part of human nature to seek approval and feel valued. Most managers find it easier to blame than to praise, and most organisations operate on the basis of only giving feedback when people have done something wrong. One of the most effective ways of improving employee wellbeing is to help staff to understand why, when and how they should acknowledge other people's contributions. Saying 'thank you' and appreciating a job well done shouldn't become a 'have a nice day' meaningless automatic response. It should be an appropriate and specific acknowledgement of a valued contribution. And remember, this is not just something that managers or supervisors do. All employees can recognise and appreciate the work of others, whether they are colleagues, members of their team or their bosses. The important thing is that it's meant sincerely and done in an appropriate manner.

Recruitment and Selection

A company's recruitment policies and processes play a major role in employee wellbeing, but their influence is often missed. We tend to view recruitment processes in terms of attracting and selecting the right person for the job. We are, quite rightly, concerned primarily with performance. However, there is a danger in this approach when performance is exclusively linked to the ability to do the job. How many recruitment processes also take into account the ability to enjoy the job and fit in with the organisational culture and values? Recruitment processes that focus on tight selection criteria may well miss the misalignment of values or basic individual needs that make the difference between a good and a bad fit to the organisation, between a healthy and an unhealthy employee.

Call Centres

A simple example of this misalignment is found in the growth area of customer call centres. In the UK, there has been an explosive growth in the number of people working in telephone response centres, customer service centres or call centres. Some of these are run and managed by a supplying organisation such as a phone company or a direct mail supplier. Others operate on a contract basis, with their staff providing an order-taking or a help-desk service for other organisations. In addition, some of the call centres will work for a variety of organisations and take overflow calls at times of high demand.

One large organisation employing several thousand people in a number of call centres looked at the recruitment process and identified the need for good social skills as one of the selection criteria. The recruiters thought that because the job involves spending all day talking to people on the telephone they should select people who are sociable and enjoy talking to others.

Unfortunately, the nature of work in many call centres precludes contact with anyone other than the person on the end of the phone. There is little opportunity for social interaction, talking to people and building relationships. Even the interaction with the callers doesn't use the social skills that were identified as a key criterion in selection. The computer screen drives the conversations with the customer and there is pressure on the call centre operator to deal with the customer's query as quickly as possible and be ready to move onto the next call. There simply isn't the opportunity to engage in any normal social interaction either with colleagues or customers. Our research in this organisation found that one of the major reasons for the high levels of staff turnover in their call centres was a feeling of isolation and a lack of social support. The recruitment process selects people who are friendly, outgoing and sociable and puts them in an environment where they spend all day without any meaningful interaction. These people are good on the phone, they are polite and well mannered and appear friendly to the callers. Unfortunately, the skills and personality characteristics that make them good at their job means that they feel isolated and lonely at work. Under these circumstances it's not surprising that people find the work soul-destroying and leave as soon as they can.

Values Mismatch

Another example of the impact of inappropriate recruitment and selection on employee wellbeing occurs when there is a mismatch in values. We have seen many examples of this in organisations. There is the production operator with a strong belief in quality who is forced to work in an environment where 'getting it out the door' is the only thing that matters. The sales person who believes that business should be conducted fairly, but has to work in an environment that uses underhand or manipulative sales practices. The secretary who has to cover for her boss about why reports haven't been written, meetings haven't been attended and so on. These mismatches in terms of what we want from work and the way our values reflect those of the organisation are often ignored, either because they are not seen to be part of the recruitment process or that the understanding of employee wellbeing is not well developed within the business.

This failure to recognise the psychological and social fit between the individual and the workplace provides further evidence of the need to raise the profile of these aspects of workplace wellbeing. Although many recruiters may miss differences in values or in aspirations, most of them would spot a physical mismatch. Employers are usually quite good at recognising that somebody who is involved in physically demanding work needs to be physically capable of doing it. They don't always apply the same principles to people involved in a psychologically demanding role.

There is an old saying, recruit for attitude and train for skill. Attitude is not just about motivation or the desire to succeed, it's about what the prospective employee wants from work.

Fitness for Work

People change and jobs change. Even when steps have been taken to recruit the right people into the right job in the right working environment, it's still possible to put people into a situation where their wellbeing suffers. The physical, social and psychological needs of the individual may have been matched to those of the job and the organisation at the time they were recruited or promoted, but it won't always stay that way. Things may happen to the individual that affect their suitability for the work and it's not safe to assume that just because somebody was suitable for the job when they were recruited that that situation will continue indefinitely. Their 'fit to the job' should be reviewed on a regular basis. From the individual's perspective, when the change in work is physical, it's fairly easy to see that there may be problems, and for both the employee and the manager to recognise that this may be leading to ill health. This is much more difficult in a situation where the changes are psychological or social. If, for example, the volume of work has changed or the technology has become more difficult to understand, or the level of service required is higher, then this may be placing excessive pressure on the individual. This change may happen so gradually that neither the individual nor their manager is aware of the problem until it reaches critical levels.

Increasing Demands at Work

In our workshops on employee wellbeing, we illustrate this problem with a short demonstration of the impact of changes in the workplace on the employee. We ask a couple of people to come forward and take part in a job that involves them holding a tray. We use a two-handled tray and show that both people can hold it quite comfortably with little obvious strain or discomfort. We explain that as time goes on, work gets more demanding and that just holding the tray is no longer enough. We add books and paper to the tray to make it a bit heavier, making the job a bit more difficult. We then explain that the business is now finding itself in difficulty and that we actually only need one person to hold this tray, so we make one of the people redundant. The person left holding the tray is now doing the work of two people. It's a little more uncomfortable but they can manage. They adapt to the new situation, perhaps by changing the way they hold the tray, and continue to demonstrate that they can carry out their responsibilities. We then explain that, as time continues, we need to raise productivity and we put more papers on the tray. At some point, the tray will become too heavy to hold and the person will have to let go.

The point of the exercise is that with a physical, demanding job like holding a tray loaded with books and paper, you can start to see when it's getting difficult and the individuals themselves do not feel embarrassed about saying that they need some help. When the pressures, the demands placed upon people, are psychological, it's much harder to tell that the employee is being damaged and much more difficult for them to admit that they need help. Managers therefore need to be able to monitor what's going on with their people, observe how they're being affected by the changes in the workplace and recognise before it's too late when they might need help.

Job Design

The importance of good job design is an essential component of employee wellbeing. Research shows that jobs that are boring, repetitive and provide little opportunity for control or influence can be very damaging to employees. Organisations need to regularly re-evaluate what they are trying to achieve and how their organisational structure helps achieve its objectives. It may be possible to change the way that jobs are designed so that it becomes easier to achieve the organisational goals and improve employee wellbeing. We can use the win-win approach to ensure the optimal balance between individual and organisational goals.

We need to look at every job in the organisation and ask two simple questions: can this be done more effectively, and can it be done more easily? The drive for improved efficiency and higher output has concentrated on increasing productivity and, more specifically, short-term productivity. It didn't seem to matter if people were burnt out, as long as the business could squeeze a little extra profit from them. In many cases marginal improvements in output or short-term unsustainable gains were made at the expense of employee wellbeing. Once again we come back to the financial justification. If firms cannot put a price on wellbeing and people are a cost centre not a profit centre, then any calculation will be distorted and result in a decision that sacrifices the worker.

The End of the Job

The problem with trying to improve job design is that, in the modern workplace, jobs are becoming obsolete. This doesn't mean that work is disappearing, just that the traditional notion of the job as something that can be specified is an outmoded concept. For many years, enlightened human resource professionals have been critical of job specifications. The standing joke is that if organisations were to insist that their employees stuck to their job descriptions, the organisation would collapse in a short time. The threat to 'work to rule' used by trade unions as a bargaining counter in negotiations was a powerful weapon to use against the employers. Most managers know that if their staff only did what they were supposed to do, very little would get done. There is little room in the modern organisation for jobs. People working in organisations are expected to work on a variety of tasks. They give their maximum contribution to the business and gain maximum benefit for themselves when they are multi-skilled, flexible and adaptable. Organisations that believe that jobs can be rigorously defined and tightly controlled are ignoring the changing nature of the workplace and the growing demands for freedom and flexibility. An organisation keen to improve employee wellbeing will not rely on job descriptions or job specifications. Instead they have clarity of vision and an understanding of the way individuals can add value to the organisation.

The difference between managing people by adherence to rules and specifications instead of through a shared vision and common understanding is illustrated by the instructions given to an employee responsible for cleaning a café. In a controlled environment the job specification will tell the person doing the job that at 9.00 am they need to brush the outside, at 9.20 am they should clean the work surfaces, every 35 minutes they should check the bathrooms, they should collect the litter and so on. The job description may run to a dozen pages of clear, detailed instructions, sometimes linked to performance criteria and perhaps even specifying the materials to be used. The organisation has produced a highly controlled standardised process that requires no input at all from the individual worker. The job has been specified not for a person, but for a machine. In contrast, a much simpler and far more effective solution is simply to tell the cleaner that the restaurant has to be so clean that people notice.

In a similar way, supermarkets that want to reduce the number of people in a queue can give their staff detailed instructions that tell them when they should be on the tills, what they should be doing in terms of their other duties and so on. A supervisor will be responsible for deciding when another till needs to be open and taking someone off another job to staff it. A more enlightened business would simply ask their staff 'keep an eye on the tills – if there are ever more than two people queuing, stop what you're doing and open up another checkout'. This change in approach massively simplifies the workplace and gives the individual the freedom to act. A simple straightforward test to apply to your organisation is 'Are the instructions you are giving your staff so detailed that an automaton can carry them out?' If so, throw them away; they're not giving your people the freedom to act.

This is not to say that employees do not need to have clear objectives. The ability to measure progress against a predefined target is important for self-esteem and development as well as performance measurement. Setting clear performance objectives and monitoring progress against them allows for considerably greater decision latitude and all the benefits of personal control that go with it.

Performance Management

As we said at the beginning of this book, organisations and managers are fond of saying 'people are our most important asset'. Performance management is yet another area where this statement is at odds with the reality of working life. If an organisation truly believes that people are its most important asset, then the way people treat others would be part of the performance management system and a key performance indicator for every employee. Even at the management level, few managers are actually measured and rewarded in terms of the way they treat their staff. The increase in the use of 360-degree feedback and analysis of job satisfaction levels by manager or team leader is an encouraging sign that people issues are becoming more important, but there is still a long way to go. People tend to do what gets noticed and what they get measured on. If no one cares about the way they treat other people, there is little incentive for them to change their behaviours. In most organisations the situation is even worse because performance management criteria continue to reinforce those behaviours that 'get the job done' or produce results, irrespective of the impact on people.

The Control–Demand Balance

The relationship between the amount of control an individual has over their work and the demands placed upon them is a key indicator of healthy work. Research has shown that ill health is associated with high demands and low control. When work demands increase and the individual employee's ability to control their work decreases then they become more rigid, report more pressure and feel unable to make a positive contribution to the organisation.

In contrast, those people who are under similar high demands but are able to exercise control over their work and have support from their bosses and co-workers, operate in what researchers call 'an active environment'. They are able to try different ways of doing things, acquire skills and feel they're making a positive contribution to the organisation. Although this demand control balance may oversimplify the realities of working life, the message is clear. Employee wellbeing is improved by giving people control and support. Increasing control and support leads to a more satisfied, more enthusiastic, more committed and more productive workforce. Organisations that have improved the individual's ability to influence their work have developed structures that promote self-managed individuals working in self-managed teams with flat hierarchies and high levels of participation. Participation is not just in terms of the work that people do, but also in the future direction and strategy of the organisation.

Growth and Development

Employee wellbeing is also a function of the way that people are encouraged to grow and develop at work. Much has been written about the importance of learning both from the individual and the organisational perspective. Confidence, self-esteem and self-worth are all linked to knowing that you are valued and that your contribution is appreciated and respected. A working environment that encourages people to learn, to take risks, to try new challenges is more likely to encourage people to feel good about themselves and enjoy their work. Once again, the irony is that we are discussing this as a way of enhancing wellbeing when it is clearly a major contributory factor to organisational success.

Continual Learning

Writers like Peter Senge believe that organisations cannot improve unless their people continually learn and that organisational learning is linked to individual learning. As long ago as 1960, researchers were suggesting that organisations whose employees are apathetic, unattached and uninvolved will only be successful as long as there is no competition and the organisation isn't growing. In times of change, these organisations will not be able to adapt. Rosabeth Moss-Kanter showed that companies that allow employees to learn are more able to innovate and develop new ideas than the more traditional organisations. She showed that companies able to use the creative energy of their employees are able to adapt and evolve more quickly and more effectively.

Flexible Working Hours

One of the most puzzling features of working life at the end of the millennium is that many organisations still believe that all employees should start and finish work at the same time. It obviously makes sense to ensure that machines are manned and that offices and shops are open for business at the times required by the business, but, with the exception of very small businesses where opening hours are limited by staff availability, it shouldn't be necessary for everyone to arrive for work and leave at the same time. Although it makes sense for organisations to have the majority of staff available between certain hours, it should still be possible for individuals, workgroups or departments to self-manage working hours to give flexibility to both the employee and the employer. If the relationship between manager and employee is founded on trust and mutual respect, then sophisticated flexible work schemes are not required. It is enough for the manager to know that the employee is working the contracted hours at the times required by the business without recording every minute. It is also reasonable for the employee to work the agreed hours without accumulating 'carry-over' days or staying late without actually doing anything so as to maximise their hours.

Work, like life, is about give and take. It is about finding win-win solutions that benefit both the employee and the employer. The systems for managing flexible working should be based on the principle of mutual benefit. An employee should be allowed a couple of hours off to attend their son's school assembly or let in the washing machine repairman. But that same worker should also be willing to work a couple of hours extra to complete an urgent piece of work. If both the employer and the employee understand this, there is no need for expensive and bureaucratic administrative systems to police working hours.

Another factor undermining the notion of fixed working hours is the change in employment practices so that people are paid on the basis of the contribution they make, not the number of hours they work. With the rise of self-employed contractors in all occupations, the increase in teleworking and the disappearance of traditional jobs, it makes much more sense to pay people on the value they add or the services they provide, not on how long it takes them to do it. Full flexibility comes with the freedom to choose how, where and when you work. It allows you to balance your life with your work so that the two are mutually supportive, but it also brings with it the responsibility of adding value by the work you do. As organisations become more sophisticated in their flexible work arrangements, employees should find greater freedom to balance their lives without the artificial constraints of a 9 to 5 existence. They will, however, pay a price for this freedom. They will be more accountable and more responsible for their individual contribution. Some people will find this extremely uncomfortable and both employee and employer will have to monitor the situation carefully to ensure that the new work arrangements are fair to both of them.

Values – 'The Way We Do Things Around Here'

All of these individual drivers for employee wellbeing can be grouped together to define the way that people work together in an organisation. The issues may be complex and interrelated, but they can be condensed into a few simple principles that describe and determine the way that people are treated and the way that things get done. Clearly defined and explicitly stated value statements are an essential component of workplace wellbeing. Unfortunately, far too many organisations have employed highly skilled marketing, human resource, or communication professionals to help them produce a fine-sounding set of words that are completely at odds with the reality of working in these organisations. They have the words, but their actions don't support them. For example, the organisation may talk about respect for the individual, but everyone knows that managers bully their way to the top. As a result, the values become devalued and the vision becomes a chimera. If your organisation has value statements or has defined the way that people should be treated, the first step is to find out how many people know what the values are and how many believe that they reflect the reality of working life. If there is a mismatch between the way the organisation states people should be treated and the way that people are actually treated, then quantify the gap and put programmes in place to bring the two together. Provided that your organisation's values recognise the importance of people, then taking steps to ensure that they are acted upon should have a significant impact on wellbeing.

The second principle is to make sure that the way you treat people is simple to understand and can be followed by everybody in the organisation. It's not just the senior managers that need to understand and be able to translate values into behaviours; even the most junior person in the organisation should know what is expected.

One of the best examples of how values can influence behaviour is found in the Zeneca Pharmaceuticals booklet *The Way We Do Things Around Here*. This booklet lists the key values, the way that people do things, and describes in a few words the characteristics of people that are good at this. The booklet also gives ideas to help people develop. For example, one of Zeneca's values is that 'employees are encouraged to work and communicate honestly'. The booklet says that people who are good at this can:

- admit when they have made a mistake;
- ask for views and opinions;
- tell the truth, act with sincerity;
- share failures as well as successes;
- be prepared to share information;
- trust people.

Another value is 'Treat everyone fairly and with respect'. This means that people who are good at this:

- respect people as individuals and value diversity;
- recognise people's contributions and say thank you;
- listen and respond to the feelings and views of other;
- assume that people will act with the best intentions;
- avoid blaming others.

The booklet quoted above, with permission from Zeneca Pharmaceuticals, is presented in a friendly, informative way and has been extremely well received by staff.

SUMMARY

Good management is simple in theory and difficult in practice. Wellbeing is driven by a complex and interrelated set of issues such as management style, communication, shared values and vision and all the other aspects of people management. These issues have a direct impact on employee wellbeing but are often overlooked. They are a powerful force for improving wellbeing and they can also be a major factor in destroying wellbeing. Think of the effect a change of manager can have on a group of employees. A poor people manager can destroy morale, creativity and enthusiasm in an instant.

9
Introducing Wellbeing Initiatives

WELLBEING AT WORK – WHO IS RESPONSIBLE?

Who is responsible for employee wellbeing? Is it the employee or the employer? Is health a personal matter for the individual or a legitimate concern of the organisation? In our experience the answer is very straightforward. Employee wellbeing is the joint responsibility of the employee and the employer. The employer is responsible for creating a safe and healthy working environment and providing the conditions that enable people to work in a productive and fulfilling way. The employee is responsible for their personal health and wellbeing behaviours. They should come to work ready, willing and able to do their jobs positively and enthusiastically. This combination of the healthy and happy employee finding fulfilment in stimulating and enjoyable work may sound like an idealistic dream, but that doesn't mean that the dream isn't worth pursuing. We know we have to start with the basics, the visible health issues, and, in most organisations, just getting the basics right is an enormous undertaking. However, starting with the basics doesn't mean abandoning the ideal. Any steps we can take on the road to improving wellbeing at work will bring us closer to this vision and, who knows, perhaps one day some of us will get there!

A different but no less valid question concerns the right of employers to become involved in the lives of their staff. Do employers have the right to seek to manage employee health? This is a thorny question. The answer is yes, but not if the process is punitive and the reasons are to maximise the benefit to the employer at the expense of the employee. Employers demand much from their employees and should create an environment in which people can function well and be productive. But, employers do not have the right to demand that employees change their lifestyle, give up smoking, take more exercise or build effective support networks outside of work. There is a fine line here – we recognise that the whole person comes to work, not just the bit of them that does the job, and lifestyle issues have a direct effect on the employee's ability to do the job. It seems reasonable to make a distinction between those aspects of an employee's wellbeing that affect their ability to do their job and those that don't. For example, few people would argue that employers should not be involved in helping their employees to overcome drinking or drug misuse problems when they affect their ability to operate machinery or work safely. However, it could be argued that trying to reduce social drinking outside of work, in a situation where it has no real effect on the employee's ability to do the job, is not a legitimate concern of the employer. Once again we need to come back to the person-centred approach to health and decide what's reasonable for employees in our organisation. We need to collect information on health behaviours and decide which are relevant to the business and affect the ability to do the job and which are the 'nice to dos', the things that will help the employee lead a fuller and healthier life but have relatively little impact on the workplace.

A few employees will regard any involvement in their health or wellbeing with scepticism and suspicion. Some will see it as interference. However, our experience shows that when well-being initiatives are communicated effectively and openly, the vast majority of employees respond positively to the employer's interest in their health. Even where there are a few initial 'misgivings', these are likely to be quickly overshadowed by relief at the recognition of just how much they contribute, and how hard it sometimes is to keep on contributing. Employers need to continually show that they care about and are interested in their staff. Wellbeing programmes that demonstrate this will always be well received.

The Benefit to the Individual and the Organisation

Many managers assume that improvements in employee well-being must inevitably lead to a reduction in productivity. It is an attitude that finds its extreme expression in a macho view of management, in which only the tough survive and people who can't take it are the weak failures who have to leave the organisation because they 'can't stand the pace'. In these organisations, autocratic bosses intimidate and sometimes bully their subordinates to achieve success. They have no awareness of how counter-productive this is for long-term survival.

The fear that taking action on health will reduce productivity was demonstrated at a recent presentation on the results of a stress survey. The senior managers of this organisation were expecting the worse: they knew they had some concerns, they knew they had problems with labour turnover and sickness absence and recognised that stress at work was a problem for their employees. They knew they had to do something to reduce the stress levels and assumed that any actions they would take would mean a reduction in workload or an increase in staffing and reduce productivity at a time when the business was struggling. The managers were astonished to find, when the results were presented, that far from being told to increase staffing levels or reduce overtime working, their problem was that their staff felt under-utilised and under-stimulated. Stress, in this particular case, was caused by boredom and lack of stimulation, not by overwork and too much pressure.

The other key issue to come out of the survey was that the lack of stimulation and challenge was linked to inadequate technology. The boredom and frustration was caused by employees continually having to wait while the computer systems broke down, didn't give the information they needed, or took far too long to return the results of a query. To the delight of the IT director who had been arguing for more investment for some time, the survey showed that investment in new technology would facilitate an improvement in working practices, significantly reducing non-productive time. The same number of people could then deal with many more customers, more quickly, without the stress-inducing frustration of endless delays as they waited for the machines to respond.

Organisational Commitment to Employee Wellbeing

An organisation's commitment towards improving employee wellbeing can be measured on a spectrum ranging from low commitment to high commitment. Low commitment is found in organisations that fail to address even the most basic wellbeing issues. These organisation comply with health and safety regulations and may even offer a few 'health' benefits such as executive screening medicals or private health insurance, but they do this because they have to, not because they see the advantages of a healthy workforce. Legislation requires them to protect their employees and the job market encourages them to offer health benefits to staff. In this sort of organisation, very few managers accept responsibility for health; they either ignore it or believe it's up to human resource or occupational health departments. The organisation doesn't allocate resources to improve wellbeing and it is certainly not regarded as a business issue. There are few, if any, policies on health and, where policies do exist, few managers are aware of them. The policies exist to comply with legislation, they are not regarded as relevant to running the business. A lack of commitment to managing wellbeing is also demonstrated in the managers not being interested in the subject and either unaware of, or accepting, bad working practices.

In contrast, an organisation that is highly committed to improving wellbeing makes these issues a business priority. In these organisations, employee wellbeing is the concern of the board and the chief executive takes ultimate responsibility for the people who work there. In the highly committed organisation, employee wellbeing policies will be in place, they will be regularly reviewed, written in a form that line managers can understand and emphasise the need for managers to take responsibility for managing health. The line managers are aware of the policies and familiar with the issues of employee wellbeing. They recognise that managing employee wellbeing is their responsibility and, in the most highly committed organisations, employee wellbeing will be a factor in their performance appraisal. The organisation recognises that improving employee wellbeing and reducing absence requires both human and financial resources and these resources are made available. Underlying this approach is an attitude to promote and encourage good working practices, and employees and managers are motivated to continually improve the way they work.

MANAGING BEHAVIOUR CHANGE

In previous chapters we looked at the need for change and identified those aspects of employee wellbeing that could be improved at both the individual and organisational level. This chapter focuses on the change process itself. How do we introduce wellbeing improvement programmes so that individuals and organisations will actively embrace change? In our experience, many change programmes fail because the people responsible for managing change don't pay enough attention to individual readiness to change. They design and implement well-thought-out, highly detailed, well-structured change initiatives without thinking about the reasons why people should want to change. This applies both to individual employees changing their health behaviours and to board directors deciding that wellbeing is a worthwhile investment.

We are creatures of habit; even if we feel uncomfortable with the current situation, we know that change requires effort and, most of the time, it's easier to stay as we are. In any group of people there will be some that love change, get bored with stability and will jump on board any change initiative. There are others who abhor change. They like stability and security, they like the familiar, the tried and tested. Most of us are somewhere in the middle. We want things to stay the same, only get better! Most of us need a reason to change – we need to see the benefits to ourselves, phrased in language that is relevant to our situation. If we don't know why we should change, we are left with the so what? You can imagine the conversation in the staff cafeteria on the announcement of a major reorganisation: 'The company has launched this new multi-million-pound change programme that's going to completely reorganise the way we work. So what! How does that help me?' These questions need to be answered at the start of the change programme, not halfway through the implementation when the managers responsible for the change start to meet 'unexpected' resistance.

The probability of achieving lasting change at the individual and organisational level is increased when change programmes are linked to employees' readiness to change.

The Burning Platform–Compelling Vision Model

The readiness to change model we described in Chapter 6 outlines a structured approach to managing change and suggests that, for most people, change takes a long time, usually weeks or months in each of the stages. Some changes happen more quickly and, in extreme cases, can be almost instantaneous. One way of helping people to understand how to achieve rapid change is to talk about the two extremes of the change spectrum: the need to move away from an objective and the desire to move toward an objective. This has been described by Daryl Conner, in his book *Managing at the Speed of Change*, in terms of a 'burning platform' or a 'compelling vision'.

As the terms suggest, two major reasons for rapid change are either to escape from danger or to move towards opportunity. The situation with the burning platform occurs when things are so bad, they couldn't get any worse, whatever you do is bound to be better. Conner describes how the idea came to him while he was watching a news interview with an oil worker who had survived an explosion on an oil drilling platform in the North Sea in which over 160 people lost their lives. The survivor, faced with an out-of-control fire, leapt 150 feet off the platform into the burning waters below. No one in their right mind would make a jump like that and the chances of survival were very low. When asked why he'd done it, the oil worker simply said, 'It was either jump or fry'. If he'd stayed on the platform he would be dead – any alternative had to be better.

The compelling vision is also self-explanatory. This is where the attraction of moving toward an opportunity is so great that you'd be foolish not to do it. The compelling vision is the stuff that dreams are made off. The essence of a compelling vision is captured in the film 'Field of Dreams' by the phrase 'build it and they will come'. At a trivial level, it's the reason that people buy lottery tickets and, at a more serious level, it's the reason that people like Thomas Edison devoted year after year of their lives trying to invent the electric light bulb. The 'burning platform–compelling vision' model of change helps people and organisations to understand the reasons why they need to embark on a change programme.

Change can be destructive and damaging – just because organisations and people can change, doesn't mean that they have to. It helps to understand the size of the change and the relative consequences of following a change programme. If an individual has just had a major heart attack or an organisation has just lost a major slice of its market, then they're on the burning platform. They can't stay as they are, they have to change and have to do something different. Everything else is irrelevant and the trick then is to make sure that the change process is as successful as possible.

At the other extreme, a person may be healthy, happy and comfortable with what they've got and an organisation may be successful and growing, but both the individual and the organisation see an opportunity of a lifetime that simply can't be missed. In this situation the way that change is implemented and the messages that persuade people to accept and embrace change will be very different from the ones that drive change from a burning platform.

THE RESPONSIVE ORGANISATION

In Chapter 2 we looked at the changing environment and saw that these fundamental changes have an impact on the workplace. Research into the changes in organisation structure to meet the environment suggests that bureaucratic, hierarchical organisations may be unable to cope with a business environment that requires adaptability, flexibility and a willingness to change. Our research suggests that organisations that are flexible, adaptive and supportive of their people promote individual wellbeing. Organisations that are hierarchical, controlled and autocratic damage individual health. The message is clear: organisational flexibility and responsiveness is linked to workplace wellbeing. It doesn't really matter whether good wellbeing makes organisations more responsive or if more responsive organisations promote better wellbeing. The important thing is to understand the benefits and manage the change.

Characteristics of Responsive Organisations

The three major characteristics of responsive organisations are responsiveness, awareness and the willingness to act:

1. *Responsiveness.* The organisation needs to be able to identify changing circumstances and be able to respond to those changes quickly and effectively. It needs to be able to mobilise its people and its resources to meet the opportunities ahead of its competitors. It also needs to recognise problems, closing markets, dying technologies, changing market conditions and take evasive action while less responsive competitors find themselves unable to change.
2. *Awareness.* Responsive organisations need to be aware of their environment. They need to be sensitive to changing demands and have systems in place that alert people in the business to changes in their external environment.
3. *Willingness to act.* The link between being aware of changes in the environment and having the ability to respond to those changes is the willingness to take action. Organisational inertia is a very powerful force. Even if the organisation is aware of dangers or opportunities, it's very easy for them to carry on doing things the way they've always been done. This means that awareness has to extend to the decision makers in the organisation and, as they are often the furthest removed from the customers, the information and communication systems need to be in place to make sure that they get the messages, understand the implications and take action. Once a decision has been made, the responsive organisation adapts to take the appropriate action. Without the link between awareness and response, there is only empty change.

There are organisations that pride themselves on their flexibility and their ability to change. This is excellent as long as the changes are appropriate to the changing circumstances. Sometimes we confuse adaptability with unpredictability or irrationality. Organisational change must be in harmony with the changing environment. It's possible to be responsive but respond in the wrong way, making the situation worse, not better. This is the fate of many organisations that adopt the latest management fads without qualifying the need. These businesses run with constant change that is unsettling for the people and counter-productive for the firm. A more detailed analysis of the need to change and the relevance of the change intervention may avoid unnecessary or misguided change and would free up massive resources that could be used for developing the business. Our research shows a common theme running through these types of organisation: the staff believe that there is too much change and that reorganisation is damaging the business. Even if the change is appropriate, it has not been well communicated.

THE CHANGE CONTINUUM

In Chapter 6 we looked at the wellness continuum, the way an individual can progress from ill health to fulfilment. The ends of the fulfilment continuum represent the burning platform and the compelling vision of individual health. People will change their health behaviours to move away from illness and towards fulfilment. The need to change and the enthusiasm for change will depend on where they are on the scale.

In a similar way, an individual or an organisation can move from a must change situation, driven by the need to avoid a negative, to a should change situation driven by the need to acquire a positive. Along the way, the spectrum passes through 'things could be better' to 'no real need to change' to 'nice to change'.

Steady-State Change

Wellbeing programmes usually start with a blaze of publicity, a high level of enthusiasm and initial interest and then fizzle out into indifference. In most cases it isn't the programmes that are wrong, it's the way they are introduced and the unrealistic expectation that because people say they want to improve their health and wellbeing they will take action to make it happen. Once again, enthusiasm triumphs over experience. Changing health behaviours is a long-term project; it may be better to adopt a steady-state rather than a big-bang approach and introduce initiatives that build up over time. In this way we can cater for the people who need to be persuaded to change as well as the early adopters, the ones that see the compelling vision or are on the burning platform.

Prochaska and DiClemente quote the story of a man who had been given clear instructions about how to find a particular street after he'd asked for directions. After being told the way, the man started walking in the wrong direction. When it was pointed out that he was going the wrong way, the man replied: 'Yes, I know where I should go, but I'm not quite ready to go there yet.' Intending to change is not the same as making the change. This is why so many individual and organisational change programmes fail. People think that they will do things differently but, on the whole, they don't. People resolve to keep their desk tidy, be better time managers, take more exercise or give up smoking. At the time they say they'll do these things, they believe that they will, but unfortunately they don't. One example of this is a quit smoking programme developed by a major health maintenance organisation on the West Coast of the USA. When asked about wanting to give up smoking, over 70% of the eligible smokers said that they would take advantage of a professionally developed self-help programme if one was offered. A sophisticated programme was developed and offered with great publicity. A total of 4% of the smokers signed up!

Matching the Message to the Reason

Understanding where people are on the reasons-for-change continuum helps define the message. It's obvious that if people are on a burning platform, the only message that matters is that the fire is burning out of control and if you don't jump you're dead. Why the fire got out of control in the first place and how much out of control it is, aren't important. It's a simple, powerful message, 'change or else'. If the driver for change is a compelling vision, again the message is relatively straightforward, if a little harder to get across. In this case the essence is to get people to share the vision, to see the opportunities as clearly and as enthusiastically as possible, to explain that this is what the world would be like if the vision became real.

The messages become more difficult to define as we move towards the middle of the change continuum. If there is no good reason to change, then persuading people to change can be extremely difficult. The change initiator has to be able to answer the question, 'Why bother?' If a chief executive reads a management book or listens to a speaker and decides that his organisation really ought to be more decentralised, he needs to be able to explain why. If the company is successful, growing and making money, why change? At the individual level, if someone's reasonably fit, around average weight, doesn't smoke and is a moderate drinker, there is little incentive for them to change their health behaviours.

Understanding the Why

In our work as consultants we have had discussions with many organisations about the need to improve employee wellbeing. In most cases the arguments for improving wellbeing are understood and accepted. There have, however, been a number of occasions when organisations understand and support the principle of employee wellbeing but fail to take action. The simple answer is to say that these organisations weren't ready or the timing wasn't right. What we now realise is that we hadn't understood where they were on the change continuum or appreciated their readiness to change. We assumed that because the managers said they were interested in improving employee wellbeing, they knew what they wished to avoid or what they wanted to achieve. We thought they wanted wellbeing programmes or help with implementing change. In retrospect, we can see that they were in the early stages of contemplation. Something had happened that had prompted them to start thinking about improving wellbeing and what they needed was more information, more evidence that they needed to change. Offering resources and a detailed process was too much too soon. A scoping exercise to help the organisation understand why they should consider improving wellbeing would have been far more effective.

Understanding the readiness to change state applies just as much to the internal human resource or occupational health professional as it does to an external consultant. Champions of change can quickly lose their energy and enthusiasm when faced with organisational inertia; directing their energy into delivering the right messages will be far more productive even if it means adding several months to the timetable.

The Best of Both Worlds

When we look at the reasons for change, the compelling vision or the burning platform, we have positioned them at opposite ends of a scale. In reality, these two concepts are not mutually contradictory. It's possible for an individual or an organisation to be driven by both a burning platform and a compelling vision at the same time. If this is the case, then the desire to change is at its most powerful. When analysing the reasons why people should change, first identify the primary reason and then go round the loop again to see if it's possible to find a good reason at the other end of the spectrum. If, for example, an individual has collapsed with a minor heart attack and been told that unless he starts exercising and stops smoking his chances of recovery are slim, then he's strongly motivated by fear to stop his previous behaviours. If, at the same time, he's also shown a vision of how much fitter he will be and how this will enable him to improve his tennis or enjoy skiing, then these two factors combine to provide maximum motivation.

At the organisational level, programmes to improve wellbeing may be driven by the need to reduce staff turnover because key people are leaving the business and if the outward flow continues survival may be difficult. When this desire to move away from a problem is combined with a vision of increased creativity and improved customer service, the commitment to change becomes even more compelling.

A CHECKLIST FOR ACTION – IMPLEMENTING CHANGE IN YOUR ORGANISATION

The stages of change model can be useful in planning organisational change. The following list shows the kind of actions that you could take to help influence change in your organisation:

- *Pre-contemplation.* Start to raise awareness of the need to change by discussing the drawbacks or problems with the current situation. What are the risks of continuing as you are? Are you heading for the rocks or are you missing opportunities for growth? What would a compelling vision look like?
- *Contemplation.* Collect the evidence and present it in an understandable format. At this stage it's important to provide accurate, easily accessible information that provides powerful reasons to change and highlights the risks of not changing. It is also useful, at this stage, to help people to see that change is possible. The organisation or the individual has the ability to change.
- *Preparation.* How should change be achieved? Who should be involved? What is the best way to gain commitment and share ownership? What should the organisation be doing differently? What resources are required? When should the change process start?
- *Action.* Make sure that people are doing what they said they would do, that the change process and the vision for the future are shared by all the key influencers and that people are acting together to make the changes successful.
- *Maintenance.* Monitor progress and keep providing positive reinforcement. Be prepared to change the implementation of the action plan if unexpected barriers to change arise or progress isn't as quick as it should be.
- *Relapse.* If the organisation slips back from any of these stages, be aware of what's happened and help to move the process forward again. Remember the steady-state approach and don't be afraid to re-think the strategy.

SUMMARY

Effective change management depends on doing the right things (the processes) at the right time (the stages). An organisation most needs to be able to utilise the energy, enthusiasm, innovation, flexibility and commitment of its workforce when it is fighting for survival or growing rapidly. From the individual perspective, motivational theories suggest that work is not simply about extrinsic rewards. Work also fills the higher needs for meaning, participation, creativity and security. When the organisation needs are combined with the individual needs, we can see the possibility of a clear alignment between individual and organisational objectives. This, in our view, is the true definition of the healthy organisation. It is one where the needs of the individual and the needs of the organisation are aligned in pursuit of a common purpose.

10
Making a Difference – From Strategy to Action

The previous chapters outlined a structured approach to improving wellbeing at work. Structure is necessary because the wellbeing issues are complex and interrelated. This means that the solutions will also need to be integrated, both with each other and into the organisational culture as a whole. Without a structured approach to understanding the issues and implementing the solutions, it is possible to make considerable progress in the wrong direction. We have talked a lot about gaining a clearer picture of the problem, now we need to move into action to address the issues. What do we need to do next to make a real difference to wellbeing at work?

As we have seen, a strategic approach to wellbeing can be achieved by following the basic rules for strategy development: know where you are when you start, define where you want to be and plan for how you are going to get there. Too often, interventions are introduced without a clear understanding of real employee needs and without a firm measure of the starting position. This, combined with no commonly understood target for improvement, means that the chances of evaluating the appropriateness and effectiveness of the interventions are severely limited.

The theme throughout this book is that more often than not organisations approach employee wellbeing in this way. The issue is seen as too overwhelming to manage holistically and therefore *some* progress with the symptoms will be enough. A handful of non-integrated benefits and interventions are made available to address the visible signs and the rest is trusted to luck. It does not have to be this way. As with every other complex activity, planning is everything. Taking the time to understand your starting position in employee health and wellbeing and then building a vision and road map for how to improve your position can prevent waste of time, waste of energy, waste of resource. Conversely, addressing real risks and real issues produces greater financial returns and greater employee satisfaction. Planning is all.

So where do we start? Start with where you are now.

WHERE ARE WE NOW?

Getting the Basics Right

Start with what you know or can find out easily and work forward from there. We have already talked about making quantitative data work for you, but do not overlook the qualitative information too. Make sure that you've got the basic building blocks in place before moving on to more sophisticated interventions. There is little point in implementing family-friendly working if your factory is always cold, dirty, noisy and full of fumes. You may just find that far more employees have sick children than you expected!

Figure 10.1 illustrates a structured approach to understanding these issues. This organisational health grid can be used to generate a checklist of characteristics of employee wellbeing. Take a few minutes to go through the list and rate your organisation on a 1 to 10 scale, where 1 is not really aware of the issue and so doing nothing about it and 10 is completely satisfied that you are doing all you can.

Environmental

- Safe working environment.
- Pleasant work area.

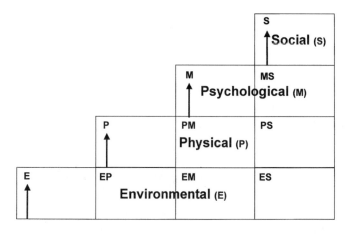

Figure 10.1   *An organisational health grid (Source: Cooper and Williams, 1994)*

- Low noise levels.
- Comfortable temperature.
- Good lighting.
- Adequate airflow.
- Absence of dust.

Physical

- Ergonomic workstation.
- Lifting and handling.
- Rest periods.
- Refreshments.
- Exercise.

Psychological

- Fulfilment.
- Self-esteem.
- Personal development.
- Reasonable pressure.
- Fair treatment.
- No discrimination.
- No harassment.
- Interesting work.
- Reasonable hours.
- Clear and measurable objectives.

Social

- Good working relationships.
- Flexible working hours.
- Opportunities to talk.
- Outside interests.
- Child-care facilities.

WHERE DO WE WANT TO BE?

Now that we have acquired a better understanding of the real meaning of 'wellbeing', the obvious answer is that 'we want to be a healthy organisation'. But when we consider how many issues are involved in being a healthy organisation, then this is clearly too broad an answer to be of practical help in making the wish a reality. But it is the right place to start. As the innate starting point for planning, articulating the mission or vision is the first plank in an effective intervention strategy.

Defining the Vision for Employee Wellbeing

The vision, or mission, is the general statement that provides the context for the strategy that will shape goals and objectives. Without taking the time to define 'where we want to be' in overall terms, it is easy for subsequent activities to lose sight of their purpose. The commercial realities of the modern workplace mean that, despite having a vision, it may not be possible to make it a reality all in one go. It may not even be possible to ever get there completely. But if a vision or overall goal has been defined, it is possible to start small, make moderate and manageable changes, knowing that those are incremental steps towards a grander plan. There is a big difference between starting small in the context of a strategy for health and starting small with no understanding of what comes next or how this one initiative can build or link with others. The overall vision provides a context and framework for all the incremental steps along the way.

If only half of what has already been said on the subject of employee health has struck a chord with you, then it is likely that you already have a mission in your mind. The issue then becomes not one of 'What will our vision be?' but of 'How do we go about communicating it?'.

Communicating the Vision

Effective communication of a vision for corporate wellbeing is vital to the whole process. It is key because in any company it is usually possible to find at least a handful of people who are sensitive to the benefits of managing employee wellbeing proactively. Unfortunately these people are usually lone voices. Where they are not, they are often hamstrung by a lack of enthusiasm towards the subject by the budget holders whose interest, of course, is a prerequisite for any action.

There is a real need, once the vision has been articulated, to encourage ownership by the most senior executives and use them to communicate and support the process as it is cascaded down through the organisation. You will not get off first base with some of the broader issues unless you can get senior management excited by the potential gain that is embedded in improved wellbeing.

The perennial question is always 'Yes, but how?' Again the work we have done with companies suggests that it is necessary to start with what you have. We have described the reasons why health matters and hopefully demonstrated that the benefits in managing employee wellbeing outweigh the required investment, so great are the costs of not acting on the issues. But it is easy to forget that this is not the viewpoint of most executives or directors. Some of them may be sympathetic to the cause, but it requires more than just a vague feeling of 'yes...that feels right' to get them to actively champion *and fund* the initiatives needed to make a difference.

To get buy-in to the vision you will need to share some of what you have found out about why a vision and road map for improved wellbeing is necessary, and how the approach will make a difference *now*. The problem with visions is that they are open to claims of utopianism. Utopianism is rarely considered to be aligned with short-term gain and this is where many managers' interests lie.

To go back to our reef analogy, there are issues that stick out above the water-line and are easy to see, such as staff turnover, sickness absence and ill health retirements. The bulk of what you need to worry about is actually below the water-line and is not easy to see. Champions for the cause will often be focused on the underlying issues, the reef hidden below the surface. However, many of the decision makers and budget holders can only see the rocks. Trying to gain commitment and funding for managing the underlying issues is likely to be more difficult than generating enthusiasm for reducing the size of the rocks! Throughout this book we have said that focusing only on the visible issues is misleading. This is true, but when it comes to building a business case you must start with the issues that are visible and costly now. Employee liability claims, litigation costs, private medical insurance premiums, long-term absence costs are real and easy to account for. If you can influence the health drivers behind these costs and in so doing reduce the drain on the profit and loss account, this releases cash back into the balance sheet. This of course is what many managers, particularly those in finance, like the most. Stretching the reef analogy still further, trying to get managers preoccupied with short-term profitability excited about managing the hidden and prospective costs of wellbeing is like trying to dive to the bottom of the reef without breathing apparatus. You and the vision will run out of breath long before you get to the bottom. Evidence of what is happening now and the cash potential in lowering those costs can give you the air in the tank you need to start working on the reef.

Where does all this lead us? Some basic principles:

- Use evidence of the visible 'cash' costs of ill health to motivate the most senior executives that the issue is big, expensive, important and commercial. It is an issue that can make or break the business and it requires focus, but it is often better to present the problem as a combination of specific and tractable issues to prevent the vision appearing 'mission impossible'.
- Take time to work through specifically what the first steps will be in making the vision a reality and how these will produce an early reduction in cash cost.

If you do these two, the following will happen almost automatically:

- Define the vision for corporate wellbeing in terms that are appropriate to the culture of the company.
- Make the vision, clear, relevant and compelling.
- Take time to understand the readiness to change issues among the colleagues you want to influence and structure the messages accordingly.
- Once they have committed to the vision, let the senior executives lead from the front and 'walk the talk'. Their behaviours must be consistent with the message.
- Communicate the vision, frequently and consistently.
- Encourage the executives who are most trusted by the employees to take the lead role in communication.
- Identify the key people who will make it happen – it is everyone's responsibility in the final analysis, but there needs to be a core group who will define the goals and monitor the roles and responsibilities of those whose objectives make the vision a reality.
- Ensure everyone else in the company knows what the roles and responsibilities are and who has them.
- Consider 'branding' the initiative – at least until it becomes truly integrated into the business culture.

Sharing the Culture – Vision and Values

Having defined the organisational culture, the next step is to explain what it means and share it with your staff. Company vision and mission statements have become something of a joke in recent years, as so many organisations have jumped on the bandwagon and written fine sounding words that bear no relation to the reality of the way people are treated. A statement of organisational values is more than a public relations exercise; it should provide a practical, meaningful declaration of what matters and the way people should work together. A corporate vision should be a beacon to guide people toward a common goal, not a paragraph in the annual report and accounts. Organisational climate and attitude surveys can provide an effective method of rating the business on the extent to which it manages according to its stated values. For example, the extent to which people agree with statements like 'the company supports me in balancing my work and personal life' could provide an indication of the way people are valued by the business.

The Corporate Culture

David Ogilvy, one of the advertising industry's most respected leaders, emphasised the importance of people and shared the key elements of the corporate culture of Ogilvy & Mather in a simple clear and elegant way. The following extract is from the introduction to working at Ogilvy and Mather given to all new recruits. We would encourage every organisation to define the way that people are treated and publish a similar reminder to their current and prospective employees – but only if they mean it!

> Some of our people spend their entire working lives in Ogilvy & Mather. We try to make it a stimulating and happy experience. We put this first, believing that superior service to our clients depends on the high morale of our men and women.
>
> We help them make the best of their talents. We invest an awful lot of time and money in training – perhaps more than any of our competitors.
>
> We treat our people as human beings. We help them when they are in trouble – with their jobs, with illness, with emotional problems, with drugs or alcohol.
>
> Gentle manners, hard work
> We are opposed to management by intimidation. We abhor ruthlessness. We like people with gentle manners. We see no conflict between adherence to high professional standards in our work and human kindness in our dealings with each other.
>
> We don't like rigid pecking orders. We give our executives an extraordinary degree of independence, in the belief that freedom stimulates initiative. We dislike issuing orders: the best results are produced by men and women who don't have to be told what to do.
>
> We like people who are honest. Honest in argument, honest with clients, honest with suppliers, honest with the company and, above all, honest with consumers.
>
> We admire people who speak their minds. At the same time we admire people who listen more than they talk, and make a real effort to understand views that differ from their own. Candour is a virtue; arrogance is not.

We admire people who work hard, who are objective and thorough. Lazy or superficial men and women do not produce superior work.

We are free of prejudice of any kind. The way up the ladder is open to everybody, regardless of religion, race, gender or sexual preference. We detest nepotism and every other form of favouritism.

There are, however, limits to our tolerance. We have little time for office politicians, toadies, bullies, pompous asses, paper warriors, prima donnas.

In promoting people at all levels we are influenced as much by their character as anything else.

(Quoted with permission from
What We Believe and How We Behave,
Ogilvy & Mather.)

HOW DO WE GET THERE?

If we now know where we want to be, the next question is how do we get there. Visions are all very well, but again there is no shortage of companies who have decided to become 'healthy' but never moved off first base. Very often the vision stays just a utopian dream in the mind of the enlightened human resource or occupational health manager. The difference in those companies where it is really happening is that clearly defined goals will have been shaped for making the vision a reality.

Defining the Goals

What are goals in this context? Put formally, a goal can be defined as an end towards which you expend some particular effort, where 'end' is a measurable result which you are prepared to make an investment in achieving. The amount of effort you are prepared to put in should always be related to the goal itself, both in terms of the direct costs of doing so and in the amount of time or money invested. In other words you need to be able to assess the cost–benefit relationship. Defining goals in employee wellbeing becomes very much simpler when there is a clear understanding of what the health issues really are. As has been said before, building cost–benefit models for a great deal of existing health investment is difficult, because there are no starting points and no goals set in the beginning, against which to measure progress. With a clear understanding of the health issues that face your employees and a sense of the true cost of those issues, then it becomes considerably easier to define the goals.

Before they are actually defined, as with any other form of business goal setting, consideration should be given to the following elements:

- *There should be a clear accomplishment to be achieved*
  What do I want the outcome to be of this activity?
  E.g., reduce sickness absence rates from 4% to 3%.

- *There should be a measurable outcome*
  How will I know when we have been successful?
  E.g., sickness absence rates were 3.9% in June and 3.5% in September.

- *Time-scale*
  When exactly do we want this goal achieved?
  E.g., reduce sickness absence rates by 25% by the end of the financial year.

- *Cost involved*
  How much investment (time or money or both) are we prepared to spend to achieve this goal?
  E.g., we will reduce sickness absence rates by 25% using our current resources and within a budget of £25 per employee for communication, training, systems development and so on.

Taking this structured approach in defining real goals at the beginning of an intervention strategy greatly increases both the chances of success and of being able to measure the extent of that success. It will be clear to all what the vision is and how the goals and their measurable outcomes relate. Because this is clear, and because the goals were appropriately defined, it will be possible to assess your progress towards your corporate wellbeing ambitions. Most importantly, it will be possible to show the cash or maybe non-cash return on each incremental step − returns which will encourage and facilitate further investment.

So vision and goals are important, but there is one more part of intervention strategy that needs to be considered. Just as a vision of workplace wellbeing will remain only a vision if there are no goals, so these goals will remain just distant targets if no objectives are defined to bring them closer to reality.

Defining the Objectives

Each goal for the management of employee wellbeing will require a set of appropriately defined objectives. Objectives in this context are the steps that need to be taken in order to achieve the goal. Picking up the strategy theme again, they are the tactics that you will employ in your overall strategy for health.

In practice, if one of the specified goals were to improve attendance management by reducing sickness absence, the corresponding objectives might be:

- Improve monitoring of current absence.
- Communicate plan for why this matters.
- Review and reissue policy on absence reporting.
- Review and revise coding systems.
- Improve ownership of the issue.
- Review and revise management information.
- Include measures of employee wellbeing in managers' key performance indicators.
- Identify key drivers.
- Collect absence data by reason.
- Perform cluster analysis.
- Identify most costly health issues.
- Influence outcomes.
- Prioritise the issues.
- Develop appropriate interventions.
- Intervene.

Vision–goals–objectives: these three thought and activity processes have underpinned every effective campaign since the beginning of time. Why should they not work for wellbeing management too?

Who Should Be Involved?

Once you have accepted the need for the management of employee wellbeing, who should do it?

As is always the case, everyone involved in achieving the goal should help in setting it. Given that corporate health is ultimately everyone's responsibility, there are clearly some practical constraints in following this ideal to the letter. However, it is involvement that is the key word here and it is necessary that as much opinion be surveyed as is practicable in order to facilitate employees and managers, at all levels, feeling part of the process.

As has been said previously, effective communication of the vision and goals is crucial to the success of a wellbeing programme. Managers and employees need a clear understanding of *why* the company thinks improving wellbeing is important and should feel involved in the processes. Without this involvement they can easily dismiss the initiatives as 'fringe' or, worse, as an exercise in the company attempting to extort even more from them by devious means.

Involvement of all parties is vital for we are, after all, talking about people. If the company takes the trouble to do all the strategic thinking, find out what the issues are and design specific interventions or support service to address them, but the employees do not feel part of the process, then why should they feel motivated to draw on what is provided? In the worst cases we have seen, much of the groundwork is done and significant steps are made to provide support for employees, but the overall effect is that the work done is of no value. Employees were not involved in the development of the vision and goals so consequently had no investment in the outcomes. Involvement is key because many of the initiatives that are ultimately put in place to support the employee require them to 'do' something differently or be willing participants in a programme. This may range from making a call to the employee assistance programme, right up to commitment to give up smoking. As we saw in Chapter 9, real behaviour change is a multi-staged process, but employees are even less likely to embark on it if they are unaware, disinterested or suspicious of what is being offered.

The Hierarchy of Health

We have already discussed the need to understand the relationship between illness and wellbeing and the importance of moving away from a traditional focus on avoiding illness towards positive health and wellbeing. Managers working in large organisations with human resources and occupational health departments tend to believe that responsibility for employee wellbeing rests with these specialists and isn't really their concern. Although the HR and OH professionals have an important role to play in shaping policy, advising and training line managers, the responsibility for employee wellbeing must lie with the individual manager. Managers are responsible for their people. This responsibility starts at the top of the organisation and cascades down through the management hierarchy. Senior managers are accountable for the wellbeing of their part of the organisation and should monitor the ability of their managers and supervisors to manage their staff on a regular basis.

This accountability once again emphasises the point that employee wellbeing is a central concern of the business. What gets measured, gets noticed. The best way to achieve this is to make employee wellbeing part of each manager's performance targets. If a manager is targeted on traditional performance issues such as sales revenue, production output, quality standards or customer service levels, she or he can safely ignore all the good words that come from HR, OH or the Board about the fact that people matter. It is inconsistent for a business to claim that it puts people first and then ignore the measurement of the people factors in the performance appraisal process. The quality of people management and its impact on employee wellbeing should also be a significant factor in the selection and promotion processes.

The Role of Human Resource and Occupational Health Professionals

In many organisations, unfortunately, the HR professionals appear to be missing many of the core people issues. They have become so concerned with administration and process management that they have completely lost sight of the needs of the people working in the business. In too many organisations, employee wellbeing has come to mean compliance with the health and safety policy or administration of the sickness absence scheme. People are not seen as individuals but as statistics to be reported to the Board, in the same way that stock levels, creditor days and the wages bill get reported. The employees echo this attitude themselves: 'We're not seen as people, we're just a number, a unit of production.' Instead of looking at people as a collection of individuals with different needs and aspirations, employees are seen as numbers on a spreadsheet. They come to work to be shaped by policies and managed by processes.

In a few organisations, the challenge of managing people as people has been taken up and championed by the OH teams. In an organisation that is fortunate to have an OH department, especially one managed by a professionally qualified OH physician, then employee wellbeing should already be an important item on that company's agenda. Some of the most forward-thinking OH departments, such as the Corporate Health Management team at SmithKline Beecham, lead the organisation in building programmes around work–life balance, resiliency and personal development. They have shown and are continuing to show the link between a healthy workforce and organisational success.

In our experience, the ideal combination is when OH professionals work together with the HR and organisational development (OD) specialists to produce interventions that utilise the experiences of both disciplines. These interventions need to be owned and implemented by the line managers and supervisors under the direction and guidance of the professional advisers. In these situations, the OH or HR teams may identify a need, perhaps through observing the extreme cases, the outcrop of rocks from the reef, where problems within the organisation manifest themselves as episodes of ill health. Alternatively, the need to intervene may come about as the result of a formal structured health audit: data collected from health risk appraisals or from observation or discussion. Occupational health physicians and nurses have the skills to recognise the problems and the tools to see whether this is an issue for one individual or something that affects a workgroup or even the business as a whole.

Once the issue has been identified, it can be discussed with the other professionals and the relevant line managers and, if appropriate, investigated in more detail. If the issue is found to be worthy of further action then the OH, HR and OD professionals can work together with line management and the affected employees to produce appropriate interventions.

The Role of the Line Manager

We have repeatedly emphasised the influence that line managers have on employee wellbeing. Many line managers will find the active promotion of wellbeing and health a real challenge. Many would argue, probably quite rightly, that they have enough problems managing their own health and wellbeing let alone that of other people. Although it may be difficult, and for some people very uncomfortable, this doesn't mean it shouldn't be done. Getting line managers and supervisors involved and thinking about the wellbeing of their staff is actually a very good way of getting them to improve their own health and wellbeing.

It is often said that the best way to learn something is to teach it and, in our experience, getting managers to appreciate staff wellness starts them thinking about their own health behaviours. Telling managers that wellbeing is their responsibility is relatively straightforward but, in isolation, will only make the manager feel that more responsibility is being heaped on their shoulders. What's needed is a programme of education, development and awareness where managers are helped to see that employee wellbeing is a legitimate part of their management role and that it doesn't mean they have to become an armchair psychologist, a first-aider, a counsellor or a physician. What it does mean is thinking about each of their employees as an individual and considering their wellbeing and welfare.

Think about what it would be like in your organisation if each manager and supervisor took a few minutes every day to think about individual wellbeing issues: 'Is John still cutting down on his smoking?' 'Did Jeff walk to work this morning?', 'Did Joanne stick to her healthy eating plan?', 'Has Sally taken some advice on her mortgage repayments?' Many good managers do this instinctively. They haven't been taught to think about employee health, but they know it's good practice to know the people that work for them – as people, not as units of production!

As always with managing employee wellbeing, there is a fine line between interest and intrusion. The vast majority of us would be uncomfortable if our boss suddenly started asking whether we'd had bran for breakfast, how much we'd had to drink the night before and whether we'd taken 30 minutes of physical exercise. The good thing about an integrated strategy for health is that it provides a frame of reference and a context for talking about individual health behaviours. It means that managers can be supportive of the health messages and encourage their people to take part in employee wellness programmes, but also means that they can monitor progress and try to help their people stick to the behaviour change. At its most basic, a concern for wellbeing could be demonstrated by making a point of using the stairs instead of taking the lift, providing water and fruit at meetings instead of coffee and biscuits, or encouraging staff to take a proper lunch break. Stopping people from snacking at their desks is a lot less intrusive than making them choose the healthy option at lunch, but may have a similar effect on their health.

So far, we have looked at how to plan the intervention strategy and who the key players will be in making it happen. Next we turn our attention to the type of interventions we can consider.

Primary, Secondary and Tertiary Interventions

In managing workplace wellbeing it is useful to think of interventions in terms of how they address the problem. Interventions are traditionally divided into three groups: primary, secondary and tertiary. Primary interventions are designed to remove or modify the issue at source; secondary interventions help people to deal more effectively with the problems; and tertiary interventions treat the damage already done. In designing interventions to improve wellbeing at work we usually need to employ all three approaches. For example, in trying to manage staff turnover a company may try to persuade an employee to change their mind after handing in their notice. The company could promise more money, a promotion or a better car. These are tertiary interventions, the damage has been done and the employee is leaving; the objective is to identify what needs to be done to persuade them to stay. An example of a secondary intervention is to encourage people to raise issues of concern before they get to the point of leaving. Training programmes, performance reviews, career progression plans can all help the employee to deal more effectively with the issues that may be influencing them to leave the firm. Although secondary and tertiary interventions have their place, they tend to deal with the symptoms not the sources. They can often be a case of too little too late. The most effective way to deal with workplace wellbeing is at the primary level. Some examples of primary interventions would be programmes designed to improve the underlying issues that influence retention. Some of these could be fulfilling work, good working relationships, a supportive manager, flexible working, attractive salary package and so on.

Although primary interventions are the most effective, they can be difficult to design and take longer to implement. Almost by definition they are dealing with issues where there is often no visible manifestation of the problem. As we have said already, treatment is a failure of prevention, but at least it is visible and can be measured. When problems are dealt with at source, so that there is no need for treatment, it is much more difficult for the organisation to see the benefit. If, following our previous examples, the employee is persuaded to change their mind about leaving, there is an immediate and obvious benefit from the intervention. If introducing flexible working meant that the employee never had the child-care problem that started the cycle of dissatisfaction, the effect isn't immediate and it certainly isn't obvious. At the end of the year, changes in staff turnover will show a decrease but many organisations either don't wait that long or lack the ability to measure change. The problem with primary interventions is that success is marked with a non-event.

The Strategic Approach to Employee Wellbeing – A Six-Step Process

Throughout this book we have talked about the need to adopt a strategic rather than a tactical approach to employee wellbeing. We have advocated a structured approach to the issue in order to overcome some of the obstacles to and misconceptions about the process of tackling employee health 'in the round'. The key steps in the process are summarised here, to focus attention as we draw to a conclusion.

Preplanning.   Select and brief the team of people who are to be involved in the planning process and communicate the vision, goals and objectives to all employees — ultimately everyone is involved in implementing the interventions.

Data collection.   Start with the obvious health-related data — sickness absence rates, health insurance claims, litigation cases and costs, long-term sick cases, ill health retirements, counselling service management reports — all the health data you have currently. Next, look at attitude survey or other employee satisfaction data: what do you know about the morale and satisfaction levels of your employees? Then add in information about staff turnover: how many people are leaving, from what job categories, for what reason? How many would you have preferred to keep? What about recruitment data: is it easy to replace staff, how long are jobs left unfilled, are there key shortage areas? In addition, consider the use of specialist audits for both physical health and mental health risks. These will round out the picture and add vital information about prospective health risks as well as current and retrospective health problems.

Analysis.   What does all this data mean? How does it all fit together? What are our issues? Turn raw information into knowledge by getting specialist help if necessary. How do we compare with other organisations? Benchmark with other companies if possible. Which health problems account for the largest number of days taken for absence? Which health problems appear to carry the largest direct costs? Which ones are most likely to involve significant indirect cost? Can we isolate and combine data about specific areas of the organisation that may indicate vulnerability? For example, one company had average levels of staff turnover and no overall problems recruiting. Closer analysis of the data showed that the proportion of highly skilled scientists leaving the business was far higher than for other groups, but had been hidden from view because of the way that the data was aggregated. The more detailed examination also showed that recruitment of scientists took longer, was more expensive and, quite often, jobs were left unfilled because suitable replacements were not available. The business was losing one of its most valuable resources without senior managers being aware of the long-term implications if this trend continued.

Building the vision, goals and objectives.   You know now 'where you are'. Decide now where you want to be. What are the key health issues that are driving your biggest health costs, direct or indirect? What interventions can you employ to influence the situation? Agree the health issues you plan to tackle and set the goals. Articulate and communicate the vision and the plan of campaign. Remember, if you are using absence rates as a future evaluation benchmark, that the rates may go higher as more managers focus on the need to collect data properly. Ensure that the interventions are integrated with one another. Most importantly, start at the place most likely to produce a clear and rapid pay-back for your organisation and use measurable small successes to build commitment and enthusiasm for further investment in subsequent phases.

Implement interventions.   Put the intervention plans into action. Revitalise, reposition and relaunch existing health investments. Making progress in employee wellbeing is not always about spending more money. Good interventions may already be in place, but are they targeted at the wrong risks and problems? Do they not achieve their full impact because they are fragmented and unrelated? Employee participation is the key to ensuring that employee involvement is maximised through communication and feedback loops.

Evaluate.   Review the key performance indicators that you set. How are you doing? Assess employee attitudes towards health as well as the more easily measurable factors such as absence days. Review the interventions. Are they working well, for both the employer and the employee? Review the goals. Are they still appropriate? Amend the plan as necessary and set a date when you will audit again.

THE BIG QUESTION – 'SO WHAT?'

So many times people prepare a carefully developed, well-reasoned argument for investing time, money and resources in a new initiative, only to have their ideas thrown out because other decision makers don't accept the basic premise. You can hear the words: 'We've seen the proposal, it's well put together and the arguments make sense but so what? We've got more important things to consider, why do we need to bother with this? Why does wellbeing at work matter?'

It matters because people are your most important asset, they are literally the lifeblood of your organisation. Remember the people capital of your business. Without people the only value in the business is the fixed assets – people turn assets into profits. The difference between selling off the assets and selling the business as a going concern is a crude estimate of the value of your people. What is that worth to your organisation?

So what's the bottom line? What can I do right now to get the ship better equipped to make it through the reef? Here are eight suggestions:

- Start to measure. Start to collect data and think about what you already know about your people.
- Start to make a chart. Gather together every bit of information you have that may just tell you something about employee wellbeing, and post it up on an office wall. Invite managers, co-workers and even your visitors to add bits they think are relevant. Then take some coloured string to make connections between the items. Involve people in discovering what you know, what you don't know and what you need to know. Improving wellbeing isn't work, it's fun!
- Think about regeneration and renewal, not reorganisation. Good management involves putting energy into the business and letting your people amplify that energy for productive gain. Value diversity in attitude and approach and avoid organisational entropy, the heat death of the business where individual sparkle settles into dull compliance with the status quo.
- Throw away job descriptions, people specifications and any piece of paper that treats people as units of production or as mindless automatons.

- Catch people doing something right. Praise don't blame, but do it properly and don't be afraid to say what you think. Act with integrity,
- Think about improving wellbeing at work in the same way that you think about improving customer service. The overall integrated rigorous approach works for both. So, set goals, gather information, identify the key issues facing your people and react quickly and flexibly to manage these issues.
- Do more of what people want and less of what people dislike.
- And remember: take care of the people and the people will take care of the business.

FIND YOUR OWN WAY

When we started to write this book we intended to make extensive use of case studies from the hundreds of organisations, many of them household names, that we've been fortunate to work with over the years. We wanted to share best practice and show how individual organisations had approached improvements in wellbeing at work. As the writing progressed, we realised that the case studies were a distraction, they missed the point. It's not so much what best practice organisations do that matters, it's the spirit in which they do them. Sadly there are no silver bullets or easy answers or a ten-step plan that guarantees improved wellbeing. There is an approach, a methodology that provides the structure to our work, but each organisation is different and each is different in a different way. What works for one organisation wouldn't work for another. We need to learn from others, distil the essence of their achievement, and apply the insights we have gained to our own situation. There are no charts to mark the route, only basic principles to help us find our own way.

The Message...

Think again about the sailing ship on its voyage of discovery. We can see our destination, the tropical island that lies, half-hidden, behind the spray from the ocean breaking over the rocks of the reef. We know that a safe landing will be difficult and that the swirling water and the outcrops of coral are a warning that we need to be careful. We also know that the real danger lies, hidden from view, below the surface. As we sail toward the island we need to find out as much as we can about the hidden dangers and try to anticipate problems while keeping away from the obvious hazards. As we move ahead, we take soundings and change course on the basis of what we discover about the landscape below. We choose our moment to sail over the most treacherous part of the reef and, with the help of a high tide and a watchful and responsive crew ready to change course at a moment's notice, we sail through the dangerous waters to land safely on the shore.

Improving wellbeing at work is a journey, not a destination. There are islands along the way where we can rest and recover, but the journey continues and every day brings fresh challenges. Every stage of the journey is different and there are no detailed charts to guide us. We have to rely on basic principles and keep a constant and careful lookout so that we can anticipate and react to the dangers that lie ahead. We need to make sure that our people are committed to the journey and that they understand that everyone is travelling together to the same place. They should realise that they all depend on each other and there are no passengers. Everyone has a role to play and success comes from people who are alert, flexible and innovative, and who work together as a team. We need people who are not afraid to make mistakes, who give and gain respect, and who are open and honest with others.

Improving wellbeing at work isn't easy – it requires commitment, persistence and an unshakeable belief that people matter. We have shown that employee wellbeing is a key factor in organisational success and that it is not a peripheral activity to be devolved to occupational health, human resources or welfare. The wellbeing of people should be a key performance indicator for all managers and supervisors and overall responsibility for organisational wellbeing should rest with the Board and the chief executive officer. We accept that wellbeing at work is a complex and multifaceted issue for which there are no simple solutions. There are, however, basic principles of good management that if applied appropriately will simultaneously improve both individual wellbeing and organisational effectiveness. Wellbeing is a strategic issue that can be best achieved by finding out what's going on, analysing the situation, and taking action to make things better. Measure–analyse–intervene, but always begin with the end in mind. Remember, healthy and fulfilled people create organisational success.

In the final analysis we may not have an option but to work harder and smarter at maintaining employee wellbeing. As has been demonstrated throughout this book, the cost of poor wellbeing is far higher than we can even start to account for. Incremental performance improvement, each year, every year, is a permanent requirement. To achieve this, companies can no longer afford to have employees on full pay but making a partial contribution. After all the restructuring, reorganisation and re-engineering, the only place left to look for increased productivity is in reducing the amount of employee downtime in all its manifestations.

But the issue is broader than just loss reduction. In thinking about wellbeing, the target should not focus merely on lowering the amount of wasted time, wasted energy, wasted money or whatever commodity you use to measure. Improving wellbeing releases the power of the people back into the business for positive gain, it does not just reduce the losses. It is generally understood that most people only reach a small proportion of their true potential. The factors that hold them back are often closely aligned to low self-esteem, low self-belief or simply just a lack of involvement. If there is so much untapped potential out there in your workforce, what would it be worth to release even a tiny fraction of that back into your business?

We are continuously developing our strategies for improving wellbeing at work and are therefore always interested to find out more about approaches that have worked well, as well as ones that may not have been so successful. If you would like to share your experiences, or wish to learn more about the consultancy services, attendance management systems, health risk appraisal tools and employee development programmes that we are able to offer, then please contact us:

Dr Stephen Williams
Resource Systems, Claro Court, Claro Road, Harrogate, England HG1 4BA
Phone: + 44(0)1423 529529; email: Steve@stressweb.com
Internet: www.stressweb.com

Lesley Cooper
IHC Strategy Ltd, Newspaper House, 16–18 Great New Street, London, EC4A 3BN
Phone + 44(0)171 353 4099; email: LesleyIHC@aol.com

Bibliography and Further Reading

Baruch, Y. & Nicholson, N. (1997). Home, sweet work: requirements for effective homeworking. *Journal of General Management*, **23** (2), 15–30.

Blanchard, K. (1983). *The One-Minute Manager Series*. London: Fontana.

CBI (1997). *Managing Absence — In Sickness and in Health*. London: CBI Publications Unit.

CBI (1998). *Missing Out — 1998 Absence and Labour Turnover Survey*. London: CBI Publications Unit.

Conner, D.R. (1992). *Managing at the Speed of Change*. New York: Villard Books.

Cooper, C.L. & Williams, S. (Eds.) (1994). *Creating Healthy Work Organizations*. Chichester: John Wiley & Sons.

Fingret, A. & Smith, A. (1995). *Occupational Health — A Practical Guide for Managers*. London: Routledge.

Firth-Cozens, J. (1995). *Employees' Heath and Organisational Practice*. London: Institute of Business Ethics.

HSE (1998). *Self Reported Work Related Illness in 1995*. London: HSE Publications.

Handy, C. (1990). *The Age of Unreason*. London: Arrow Books.

Industrial Society (1994). *Managing Best Practice 6 — Managing Attendance*. London: The Industrial Society.

Industrial Society (1997). *Managing Best Practice 32 — Maximising Attendance*. London: The Industrial Society.

Institute of Personnel Development (1995). *Occupational Health and Organisational Effectiveness*. London: IPD.

Institute of Personnel Development (1995). *People Make the Difference*. An IPD discussion paper. London: IPD.

Kogan, H. (1997). *The Corporate Healthcare Handbook*. London: Kogan Page.

Layton, S., Hurd, A. & Lipsey, W. (1995). *How to Plan Your Competitive Strategy*. London: Kogan Page.

Le Grand, J. & Robinson, R. (1984). *The Economics of Social Problems – The Market versus the State*. London: Macmillan.

Moss-Kanter, R. (1984). *The Change Masters – Corporate Entrepreneurs at Work*. London: George Allen & Unwin.

Nicholson, N. (1977). Absence behaviour and attendance motivation: a conceptual synthesis. *Journal of Management Studies*, **14** (3), 231–252.

Ohmae, K. (1983). *The Mind of the Strategist*. London: Penguin.

Prochaska, J.O. & DiClemente, C.C. (1983). Stages and processes of self-change in smoking: towards an integrative model of change. *Journal of Consulting and Clinical Psychology*, **51**, 390–395.

Rose, G. (1992). *The Strategy of Preventive Medicine*. Oxford: Oxford University Press.

Rosen, R.H. & Berger, L. (1991). *The Healthy Company – Eight Strategies to Develop People, Productivity and Profits*. New York: G.P. Putnam's Sons.

Rouillard, L.A. (1994). *Goals and Goal Setting – Planning to Succeed*. London: Kogan Page.

Senge, P.M. (1990). *The Fifth Discipline – The Art and Practice of the Learning Organization*. New York: Doubleday.

Stationery Office (1998). *Social Trends 28*. London: The Stationery Office.

Williams, S. (1994). *Managing Pressure for Peak Performance*. London: Kogan Page.

Williams, S. & Cooper, L. (1999). *Attendance Manager – Absence Mapper Software*. Harrogate, UK: Resource Systems IHC.

Index